SECRETS OF A FORMIDABLE DATER:

Change Your Dysfunctional Dating Patterns to Find a Quality Partner

by Saskia Kalwinek

© 2024 by Saskia Kalwinek

All rights reserved.

No portion of this book may be reproduced in any form without written permission from the author, except as permitted by Australian copyright law. For permissions contact: info@loveempowermentclinic.com.au

This publication is designed to provide accurate and authoritative information in regard to the subject matter covered. It is sold with the understanding that the author is not engaged in rendering legal, investment, accounting, or other professional services. While the author has used their best efforts in preparing this book, she makes no representations or warranties with respect to the accuracy or completeness of the contents of this book and specifically disclaim any implied warranties of merchantability or fitness for a particular purpose. No warranty may be created or extended by sales representatives or written sales materials. The advice and strategies contained herein may not be suitable for your situation. You should consult with a professional when appropriate. The author will not be liable for any loss of profit or any commercial damages, including but not limited to special, incidental, personal, or other damages.

Book Cover and eBook Formatting by Saskia Kalwinek
Edited by Alison Gray and Gila Green
1st Edition 2024

eBook ISBN: 978-1-7635798-0-4
Hard Cover ISBN: 978-1-7635798-1-1
Paperback ISBN: 978-1-7635798-2-8
Audiobook ISBN: 978-1-7635798-3-5

Visit the author's website at www.loveempowermentclinic.com.au

Contents

INTRODUCTION AND ACKNOWLEDGEMENTS 5

Part I: Dater Know Thyself 13

    Chapter 1: Attachment Styles and Dating 15

    Chapter 2: Understanding Self-Esteem 29

    Chapter 3: Handle Rejections Like a Pro 41

    Chapter 4: Idealization and Dehumanization in Dating 47

    Chapter 5: Barriers, Boundaries and Boundarylessness 55

    Chapter 6: Behavioral Mechanisms
and Partner Choice Patterns as Childhood Influences 63

    Chapter 7: Crash Communication Course 81

    Chapter 8: Social Skills Curriculum 93

    Chapter 9: Dodge the Dating Burnout 101

    Chapter 10: Types of Relationships
for Your Consideration 111

Part II: Dating from A to Happily-Ever-After 121

    Chapter 11: Meet Your Date 123

Chapter 12: Masters of Pickup 141

Chapter 13: Dating Social Skills Curriculum 149

Chapter 14: First Date and Early Stages 157

Chapter 15: Intimacy and Sexuality
in Early Stages of Dating 171

Chapter 16: Be Aware of Ghosting Realities 183

Chapter 17: Handling Tricky Dating Situations 191

Chapter 18: Can You Bleach a Red Flag? 201

Chapter 19: Green Flags and Final Accounting 237

Chapter 20: What if We Could be More than Dating? 249

References 255

INTRODUCTION AND ACKNOWLEDGEMENTS

Although dating it's sometimes portrayed as the silly side of human interactions that is usually described in girly magazines. With this book, I would like to show that there is a greater philosophy connected to it and we should not take dating lightly, but rather study it so that we can gain a quality life partner in the future.

Don't we all feel disappointed when we get our hopes up about a future relationship with our dates and there's not enough chemistry? Or when there is chemistry, but the person is incompatible or not good for us? It's hard enough to find someone fitting for a long-term commitment and additional obstacles such as our own shortcomings when it comes to mindset, attitude, vigilance, and knowledge make this goal even harder to reach. For example, dating from a place of lack, coming up with doomed self-fulfilling prophecies, second-guessing others and yourself, emotionally overinvesting, and omitting important topics that could give you more insight about the person in front of you. All of this is setting you up for failure in your love life.

I cannot control who you meet but with this book, I want to help you become the best dater you can be, so that you can enhance your prospects for a true, long-lasting, loving relationship.

I don't want to speak to you from a pedestal, even though we'll go into my credentials soon enough, so let me share some personal experiences. I used to be a horrible dater and a selfish partner, but who is a dating pro in their teens or early twenties? We all have a pattern when it comes to romantic encounters. One of mine used to be to have a few drinks to make me more fun and sociable. Unfortunately, one time this behavior got me thrown out of a bar during a date. You can imagine that there was no second invitation. For the life of me I couldn't understand why I couldn't find a long-term committed relationship. I was too self-absorbed to see the bigger picture of what I was doing wrong and who I needed to become to have a more fulfilling life and to find a good partner. I had to become the partner that I was longing for first. I needed a lot of introspection, life experiences, less alcohol, and more confidence in my social skills.

I'm assuming that you picked up this book because you can't seem to find a suitable partner either. Everyone's pattern is different, and, in this book, I'll guide you on the journey of recognition of your pattern and will point out ways for you to change it for the better. To support my claims, I'll bring up numerous psychological studies and thoughts of some of the most prominent psychologists and couple's therapists. I'll also share stories and opinions of my friends and acquaintances whom I interviewed for this book.

The first part of this book will delve into who you are as a person and a dater. These chapters ask you to consider your attachment style and how it comes into your dating patterns. Then I will teach you how to become more secure. It will help you get to know your level of self-esteem and how to adjust your mindset to increase it. I also ask you to examine your reaction to rejection and how to approach this often painful experience. We will also talk about idealizing and dehumanizing your dates and how to avoid it. Then we will refocus on boundaries and how to form them if you are lacking in this department. Parental influences will also be explored to make you realize what behavior patterns originated in your childhood when it comes to your partner choice and how you can remedy bad decision-making.

Then we'll explore communication and social patterns. There will be plenty of advice and suggestions for you to follow. We'll also discuss dating burnout to help you realize if you're heading towards it. Dating burnout can happen when you get overwhelmed by dating and start to resent others, yourself, or the whole concept of finding love. It stops you from enjoying yourself during the dating process and chases you into a corner with difficult emotions such as anger, hopelessness, or sadness. I will bring in a concept called Mindful Dating and self-care that needs to be present to combat dating burnout. We will discuss mindfulness being "right here and right now," which brings in the enjoyment of the current moment instead of having an obsessive focus on the future or the past. It's a very healthy mindset to have in life and in dating. So, you date mindfully if you're able to keep calm, enjoy the present time and not fantasize about the far future with newly met people. Lastly, we'll discuss different types of relationships that you might want to consider before you start looking for the right partner. It's important that you develop your boundaries and invest in your personal growth before you start looking for a partner, that's why the first part is so vital. I want you to have a clear view of who you are and who you need as a partner.

Part two will focus on dating from the beginning and beyond. We'll discuss how to meet a potential date and how to be around them depending on your current dating stage. While reading the subsequent chapters you can perfect your romantic social skills, learn how to progress in the early dating stages, and how to reject your dates gracefully when it's not working out.

We'll talk about tricky situations in dating, warning signs and good ones too. You'll get your final fill of strategies and pointers for future pursuits. This book also contains plenty of useful and practical exercises that you can incorporate into your life and will help you understand the presented concepts better. Lastly, we'll discuss what to do if you start to get more serious about your future with your date. I'll present you with a list of things to consider before you get into a serious relationship.

Now what is my background? And how do I know I can help you? I'm an accredited counselor and a sex therapist with a bachelor's degree in psychology. I am also a Relational Life Therapy (RLT) informed couples' therapist.

From RLT, created by Terry Real, I learned about the concept of Functional Adult state and Adaptive Child state (Real, 2022). In a Functional Adult state we can make good decisions, think logically and objectively and have the best communication. Adaptive Child state uses a different part of the brain, than Functional Adult state, which evolved before we became human during evolution. This part of the brain is called the "reptilian brain"; it's a very instinctual and preservation mechanism-oriented part of us. If we're using the Adaptive Child mindset, we're likely to fight, flight, or freeze instead of acting with courage, practicing good communication, and using our problem-solving skills. In the Adult state, however, we use a logical "human brain", called the Relational Brain by Terry Real. So, if I say "your Adult state" or "your Kid/Child state" this is what I mean by it.

I'm also an Internal Family Systems (IFS) therapist. This modality was created by Richard Schwartz. IFS has some similar features to RLT. IFS talks about having internal Parts such as inner critics, perfectionists, withdrawers, and many others that make us act or think in certain ways (Schwartz and Sweezy, 2019). The Managing Parts, such as the ones I mentioned above, conceal difficult emotions such as shame, hurt, or fear and those are called Exile Parts. Those Parts are similar in nature to what Terry Real described as the Adaptive Child state. They can be eased and unburdened through connection with Self Energy (an IFS term) which is "us at the core". In our Self Energy mode, we are courageous, calm, creative, and curious so for me this state corresponds with the Adult brain. In this book, I refer to our Adult state, a Kid/Child state, and Parts of us. I'll put forward the idea from IFS that we should be enquiring about the needs of our Parts and try to fulfill them in a healthy and mature way. For example, if your angry Part wants respect from others so it tells you to lash out, perhaps you can go another way and openly ask for respect from others in an assertive way. Or if your people pleaser Part wants you to keep the peace between you and a loved one, you can develop good boundaries that will help you become more assertive and keep the peace while following your values.

I also use techniques such as Cognitive Behavioral Therapy, Art Therapy, and Schema Therapy. These modalities help me understand my clients and challenge them to change their mindsets and lives for the better. Thanks to those approaches my clients are better able to express and understand themselves by creating art, analyzing their thoughts and behaviors, and making sense of them.

Apart from my professional development, I have also been dating a lot. My two longer and two short-term relationships and other multiple short-lived dating experiences have made me very comfortable in this field. I now interact with people from a place of confidence and genuine curiosity rather than desperation and having too many expectations. I started to enjoy, and even look forward to, the early stages of dating that a lot of people loathe. I've also realized that I chose a slightly better romantic match each time, people were more interested in me, and I had to politely reject others quite often. I had much more fun with the exploration than I used to. After such a rollercoaster of experiences I have at last found someone that I want to share my future with. All of this made me feel that I should pass that knowledge on to you!

The idea for this book began as my confidence in my life, social and emotional skills increased. I include here all the knowledge from my studies, work experience and professional development but also from my personal life and countless travels. The inspiration also came from my clients who often struggle with dating life and breakups.

Emerging dating coaches and books are an answer to all the cries for help from people who have been struggling to discover and change their dysfunctional dating patterns. Romantic relationships are the top priorities for a lot of people, so why should we treat the initial stages of a relationship as a silly game? When the idea of writing this book came to me, I was thinking "You will write yet another dating guide and that's not a serious book". But as I started to write I realized it's a book about life, self-discovery, and acceptance. If you want to be better at dating and relationships you need to apply some changes, introspection, and self-improvement and I'll guide you on that journey.

Although a lot of the content gives you useful skills, strategies, and exercises that could benefit everyone, I'm also including some of my life philosophy and my take on some social dilemmas in contemporary society. An exercise that we'll be frequently going back to is a Mindful Check-In, so familiarize yourself with it and start to perform it on a regular basis. Mindful Check-In is used by many therapists; it was found to reduce negative affect, stress, and increase psychological flexibility. It also enables us to receive compassion from others and ourselves with less fear and anxiety (Viveiros, 2020). I'll present you with my adaptations of this exercise throughout the book.

* * *

EXERCISE: Mindful Check-In
Sit somewhere quiet and close your eyes. Go inside your body and listen. What are you hearing? What are you feeling? In IFS we call those voices Parts. Try to recognize where you can feel them in your body and what they're saying. Say hello, acknowledge them from a distance and you can even send them some appreciation. Breathe regularly and into your belly as you check-in. Let your Parts just "be" without judgment. When you feel that you've looked inside enough to acknowledge where you are and what you can feel in your body, to any points of contact that you feel between your body and furniture or floor. Acknowledge all sounds, smells, or other sensations. Then open your eyes and pay attention to your surroundings. Finish the exercise with a deep breath in and a long breath out.

* * *

We are not taught at school how to date and how to interact with others in the best way possible. I think we should be educated in these subjects because it often takes a long time and plenty of heartbreak before we gain solid knowledge on the matter. And even if we have plenty of experience, some individuals find it hard to change their patterns because they don't know what the good ones look like. This book aims to show you the path and empower you to stay on track and be patient.

Writing a book used to seem like an unachievable goal for me. When I was younger, I thought you needed to study literature for years to do it. I wanted to do more than therapy, but the final push came from my now ex-partner who made me realize that I can do much more than I think. I'm very grateful for that relationship because even though it wasn't meant to be, it taught me how to be a good partner and how to work on my own communication, and use all the techniques that I teach. It prepared me for something that is in fact "meant to be".

I would like to thank my friends and family who are always there for me when I need them. They created a space where I feel safe to dream, think, and analyze life in a way that I could produce this book.

My cultural background, sexual, and romantic preferences come into the picture obviously as this book is written from my subjective perspective. I will talk about psychological studies and the opinions of other specialists, but overall, I'll be presenting my take and opinions.

I'm speaking from the perspective of a heterosexual, monogamous, Polish migrant who has been living in Australia for the past decade. The book includes some insight on open relationships and homosexual ones as well because I work with people with those sexual preferences. Nonetheless, the book is focused on heterosexual and monogamous dating as this is my area of expertise.

Part I:
Dater Know Thyself

Chapter 1:
Attachment Styles and Dating

People rarely escape parental patterns without a lot of inner work, mindfulness, and practice. So, if you think that the past is in the past you might be surprised when you start to analyze your behaviors, thoughts, and emotions. We can change our attachment style depending on our choice of partner, so we'll discuss who should be looking for whom. I will also present some recommendations to improve your attachment style, so that you can have more secure relationships in the future. First, I'll describe attachment styles, then I'll explain how they come into dating patterns of people that possess them. And how should you approach choosing a partner based on your attachment style. Perhaps you have heard of Attachment Theory, It states that there are ways in which we tend to get attached to other people (Bretherton, 1992). There are four of them.

1. **Secure Attachment** – usually formed in a family that was consistently there for the child and installed this attachment style in them, this type would feel comfortable with connection, intimacy, and vulnerability when it comes to relationships. Securely attached people have a potential for good emotional regulation and communication because they're not ruled by insecurity or fear of emotional closeness. They are better able to deal with rejections and breakups than people who have the Anxious-Preoccupied Attachment Style. They're better at recognizing their feelings and needs, therefore, they are better communicators than Avoidants are.

2. **Preoccupied – Anxious Attachment** – usually formed in a family where the parent or parents were present most of the time but there were some inconsistencies with providing affection and attention, so the child had to ask for it. This type is very often preoccupied with the relationship and their partner's emotional states. They can exhibit excessive jealousy, neediness and sometimes ask for excessive amounts of attention. Nevertheless, those tendencies can vary from person to person. People with this attachment style pay strong attention to emotional cues and often think of different ways to gain more attention.

3. **Dismissive – Avoidant Attachment** – usually formed if a person is raised in a family where the parent or parents were absent or emotionally distant or abusive. Avoidants inhibit their emotions and needs. They feel uncomfortable in intimate and vulnerable situations that require emotional connection, so they withdraw from intimacy. It's also harder for them to read other people's emotional cues as they are not very familiar with emotions and their expressions.

4. **Fearful – Avoidant Attachment** – very often people with this attachment style come from pathological families that can display narcissistic traits. They alternate between Preoccupied Attachment and Avoidant Attachment Styles. Trauma in them creates a perceived need of instability, that's why they create a pushing and pulling dynamic in their relationships.

* * *

We will focus mainly on Preoccupied and Avoidants because Securely attached individuals don't have many attachment issues in relationships and Fearful people are a combination between the two outlined styles. Nevertheless, I will provide some tips for the Fearful at the end of the chapter.

Dating implications for people exhibiting Preoccupied attachment style behaviors:
This type might be prone to overthinking, internalizing, and mind reading, which is making assumptions about what others think. They also have insecure behaviors and thoughts (Levine & Heller, 2012). Especially at the beginning of the dating period, this type can be easily triggered and misread the intentions of their date.

The first few weeks of dating can be especially confusing for a lot of people. We're trying to impress our date and put on a good front, but some reality is slipping into the honeymoon bubble. We're still figuring out if and for how long do we want to enjoy the other person's company. The longer we are in this exciting and weirdly appealing state of limbo the more feelings we "catch" so the stakes get higher. We don't want to hurt the other person or ourselves. And if there's no stability, we also fail to recognize what we can ask for and what is still off limits at this stage.

It's important to understand that even though people with this attachment style can exhibit toxic behaviors, like excessive neediness and jealousy, very often they can have functional and fulfilling relationships if they choose the right partner. They very often can find security with another Preoccupied or with a Secure person who is focused on the relationship and is happy to be close emotionally. Pairing with an Avoidant person, however, is not the best idea because Avoidants will be less able to meet needs of the Preoccupied. A relationship with an Avoidant person can seem very appealing to the Preoccupied individuals because it would most likely mimic their relation with their parents as a child. We are very prone to repeat past patterns of interactions because that's want, we know best.

The Preoccupied like to have their needs met and to be reassured so it can be even harder for them to establish when they're asking for too much. Be sure to notice the changes in your body and have regular reality checks while dating. By reality check I mean to ensure that your words and actions are performed with the understanding of the other person's emotions, dating stage and external circumstances. Even though you're not in a relationship with that person, the emotions are present already, so it's okay to have a calm and constructive conversation with your date about what's on your mind. To avoid scaring your match away it's important to face those conversations in your Adult state instead of resorting to your Kid state maneuvers.

The thing that Preoccupied individuals might find very appealing because of some insecurities are unhealthy tips from magazines, friends, and even from dating coaches. The Preoccupied might find them very alluring because they're catchy and simple but they don't serve you in the long run. Here are some examples of such advice so that you can stay clear of it.

Dysfunctional "taking back control" ideas:

☞ Be mean, to keep him/her keen
Carrot and stick scenario which can work in the short term and with the right type of people who enjoy the chase and the unpredictability. But it won't lead you to meaningful connections and a good loving relationship. If you want a stable relationship, the chase and the hot and cold behavior will need to cease at some point. Very often people who like this unstable dynamic will get bored quickly with the stability and kindness of a functional relationship. Of course, you should keep your partner on their toes, but with your involvement, interesting conversations, effort, exchanges of opinions and your boundaries. If you watch out for your clinginess and make sure that both of you are reciprocating at a similar level, you will have a balanced connection. You don't need to play mind games on people who genuinely enjoy your company. They will come to you and won't want to go anywhere else.

Constantly looking over your shoulder and thinking of ways to be difficult is not good for the soul. There is a debate about men falling in love via Vasopressin related to stress and women via Oxytocin related to physical closeness and sex (Kayaaltı & Erbaş, 2021). Therefore the idea that you should stress the guy out so that he falls for you came to be on for example social media. Perhaps in some cases that's true but I can see the same in women. Some women love the ambiguity because of their attachment wounds most likely.

Look for healthy ways to challenge your dates. If you want to stress someone out with something let it be your incredible intelligence, self-awareness, wit, ambition, looking after your body and mind, your boundaries and the way you carry yourself around people. We look up to impressive people like this, we want to be around them and like them. You will keep your partner on the "positive edge" if you strive to be a "formidable force". And remember to ask for what you need and want and call your date out on their behavior if it bothers you. That can keep them positively stressed and involved.

I remember one of my friend's was trying this hot/cold approach with a guy from our workplace who was not interested in a relationship. And indeed, he was more interested for a time, especially when she took longer time to respond to his texts. But in the end, nothing came of it.

☞ Don't talk about your emotions and insecurities with people you date, leave it for when you get into a relationship because you don't want to seem clingy.

You don't have to hide your emotions from other people. If you do that, how are they supposed to get to know you and learn how to be around you? Obviously, we don't want to seem like "we are too much," especially when we just met someone that we would like to have a relationship with. So, before you have an emotional chat with your date, make sure that what you want to say and ask for is based in reality, and that you will be talking from your Adult state. Also, that you don't blame anyone but talk about your emotional experience and perhaps use an appropriate request instead of a demand.

If your date has done something or said something that makes you question their intentions or character, it's okay to raise a concern. But it's better to handle it with curiosity rather than with blame. Don't point a finger, give them the benefit of the doubt. Let them explain before you jump to conclusions. Don't assume what other people are thinking, instead ask them about it. When we have doubts and are anxious about the relation, we tend to think the worst about ourselves and about others or we go the opposite direction and idealize our dates. Don't go down that road. If you're not starting an argument and you approach the topic calmly, you can be surprised how open people can become and how much understanding they can show in return. If they respond with rudeness, gaslighting or other dysfunctional techniques you can be sure that you have only saved yourself some time because they're clearly not a good match.

My partner when we first started dating didn't send me a message on or after Valentine's Day whereas he knew that traditional things like this are important to me. And I knew that he was on a cruise and the internet was $40 per day. But you know what? It was possible. And even though we went on only 2 dates I decided to confront him because we have a good connection. I felt disappointed that random men whom I rejected and knew less time than the guy I'm actually dating remembered to wish me happy Valentine's and the person that I wanted to hear it from didn't make an effort. My mom, whom I confide in often, advised to not to make a fuss, but I felt I should. I've sent him a half joking message where I said that he had the initiative in high school to buy every girl a flower for Valentines and I didn't even get a message. At first, he tried to be cheeky and said that he knew those girls longer. So, I countered with telling him about the men I've rejected recently who managed to make an effort. From that point he not only got apologetic but showed up on my doorstep with a bunch of roses and chocolate. If I didn't talk about my disappointment nothing would have happened and I would be boiling inside. Instead, it was a great test for this relation and he has shown interest and class.

☞ If he/she can't handle you at your worst, he/she doesn't deserve you at your best.

This one became an international meme idea, because it's been used by young people going on a first date and getting wasted. This idea works when you are in a long-term committed relationship. And even then, your partner doesn't have to endure absolutely everything that you throw their way. The antidote is taking responsibility for your actions. The more toxic shortcuts you take, the further you are from a fulfilling relationship. This idea, however, applies to difficult life circumstances like illness or financial hardship. In this case partners need to support one another if one of them is going through tough times.

I used to have this unhelpful mindset. I thought that if someone likes me, they will be ok with me getting drunk on a date. The problem is we are not the same person when we are under the influence. We get obnoxious and not that communicative and attentive. In the early stages of dating, you don't know each other that well to be comfortably drunk around one other. You need to put your best foot forward also for mutual respect. I have also gone out with a guy that came to a date late and drunk. We honestly had a good connection but the compilation of his lateness, drunkenness, and repetitions of his invitations to his house didn't allow me to continue this endeavor. He was very surprised that I was not responding to his texts and asked for an explanation. I gave it to him, and I maybe would have given him another chance but instead of an apology I got excuses. Therefore, I never saw him again. You can see that I experienced this phenomenon from both perspectives. From that time, I realized that I can't be acting like this and expect people to tolerate my drunken comments and behaviors.

* * *

Remember that you can take some steps to reduce those behaviors with Mindful Check-Ins. Here is the adapted version of this exercise for the anxiously attached people.

* * *

EXERCISE: Mindful Check-In for people exhibiting Preoccupied attachment style behaviors.
Notice when insecurity comes into your body.
    What does it feel like in your body when you get insecure?
    Notice it and try to recognize it each time. Take a breath when you feel that insecure sensation. Get yourself into your Adult state and rethink the situation in a more objective way. I always encourage people to

put their emotions and thoughts on paper. Write what your inner Kid is saying and ask yourself if it sounds realistic.

Think about other ideas or perspectives which you haven't considered. For example, if you see a photo of your date with someone that could potentially be their partner, don't jump to conclusions but ask them about it. Perhaps it's their sister or brother or their ex-partner.

* * *

Dating Implications for people exhibiting Avoidant attachment style behaviors:
If you have realized that you need a lot of personal space and you feel uncomfortable in vulnerable romantic situations and would rather stick to a surface conversation, you might be an Avoidant. People with avoidant tendencies can also have functional relationships if they're not avoiding excessively, but this depends on how their partner handles their avoidance.

If you're the type of Avoidant who likes their solitude and doesn't want to change, then your perfect fit would probably be another Avoidant or someone very secure and independent. Many couples can find happiness in their loose contact and cherishing their individuality instead of hyper focusing on the relationship. But Avoidant and Preoccupied can be a recipe for a disaster if the partners aren't working on themselves. Avoidant will be the distancer and the Preoccupied the pursuer; a dynamic that's very common in couples. If the two are also very high on each of the respective scales, it can lead to an abusive and toxic relationship where one is love addicted and the other love avoidant (Mellody et al., 1992).

It's important to remember that avoiding doesn't only mean to be quiet. A lot of people that I work with are addicts. Addiction is a form of avoidance and escapism. Often difficult situations in a relationship can trigger people to perform addictive behaviors and therefore to withdraw into this other world of dopamine indulgence. Also, perfectionism or a "no worries" type of attitude can be a hidden avoidance. People with perfectionistic traits rarely make decisions or produce an outcome because nothing and no one is ever good enough. Whereas some people whom I've met didn't want to talk about deeper feelings and communication because they believed themselves to be "super chilled" and without issues.

Others will live in a world of denial and pretend. One of my ex-partners would seemingly be close and vulnerable, but he would be covering up lack of involvement with promises of future work and change. Eventually the bubble burst and he was unable to come through with what was promised. With promises, he was also avoiding the fact that his workaholism and problematic relationship with alcohol was at the forefront instead of our future together and supporting me in hardship. I dealt with this situation using my boundaries and I've put my foot down when it comes to his promises. I informed him that either he will step up and make good on those promises or I will leave. He did the next best thing and decided to leave the relationship. I don't blame him for not having the capacity for the relationship at the time. We need to let other people continue on their journey if it no longer looks like our path.

Nevertheless, some Avoidant people simply don't have enough of the "glue" (the will to maintain a relationship) to keep a relationship together, which is why they would normally pick a Preoccupied person who will have more than enough of "glue" for both. Although, to create proper connection you need mutual involvement and reciprocation. If you would like to create a more connected relationship and crave more closeness, but just don't know how to get it, I suggest you perform this adapted Mindful Check-In for people exhibiting Avoidant attachment style behaviors.

* * *

EXERCISE: Mindful Check-In for people exhibiting Avoidant attachment style behaviors.
Ask yourself:
- How does the feeling of vulnerability and openness feel in your body?

- What kind of messages can you hear when you connect to this sensation?
- What does this voice need?
- Can you fulfill those needs in some healthy way?

* * *

Very often those Avoidant types of Parts want security and soothing. Some ideas for increasing your internal sense of safety:
- Meditation/mindfulness
- Physical exercise
- Soothing touch that you can give to yourself.
- Reassuring self-talk (talk to the Vulnerability like you would to an insecure child)
- Try sharing something that is within your comfort zone and continue with something that is slightly more uncomfortable. Proceed with those types of challenges. Set a goal for every week.
- Focus on your breath and relax your muscles during difficult conversations.
- When you catch yourself holding back, acknowledge it and if possible, mindfully let go and say what you withheld even after the conversation has finished.
- Try to be more open and vulnerable with people that you feel the most comfortable with and try to include more people when you feel that you've had enough practice.
- Gather positive feedback from people. Often, we're afraid of the reactions of others but you can be positively surprised at how welcoming people can be when you open up to them.

Dating Implications for people exhibiting Fearful attachment style behaviors:
People with Fearful attachment style behaviors create a toxic pushing and pulling dynamic in their relationships, and they can be unaware of

it. They could be love bombing, which means excessively showering their partners with affection and gifts, one minute and pushing them away the next. They crave intimacy like every human being, but they're also afraid of deep stable connection because it seems unfamiliar to them. Their childhood was most likely stressful and unpredictable and there were no stable role models available (Levine & Heller, 2012).

If you see yourself in this description, there's a lot of inner work that you need to do to become a secure and stable enough partner. I encourage you to take on suggestions from the last two parts of this chapter talking about the Preoccupied and the Avoidant problems because you have a combination of their issues.

You will need to catch yourself each time before you go too far into excessive neediness and if you start to avoid your future partner. Chances are that you also have this dynamic in non-romantic relationships. Appropriate boundaries and Mindful Check-Ins will be of great help to you on that journey. I can see in Fearful type that they first go towards preoccupation with relationships and when that gets too much they will resort to addictive behaviors or other types of avoidance.

The ex-partner with workaholism issues who I've described in the last section also exhibited some Preoccupied attachment style behaviors. That leads me to believe that perhaps he was leaning towards the Fearful style. He would get quite jealous and wanting more attention during situations where there was no threat from other men. For example, when I was having a conversation with a friend of mine who is in his 50s and there was never anything romantic between us. On the same night he not only voiced his jealousy (which was actually healthy and done using good communication) but also asked me to be exclusive and that was only a 3rd date. I reassured him and ended with "We are both attractive and it's inevitable that we will encounter people who will flirt with us but at the end of the night I'll be coming home with you."

Recovering Fearful style people should be looking for someone very secure. You can learn how to communicate and be in a relationship from a securely attached person. Securely attached people won't take the "push-pull crap" from you and might even put you in your place, which will be very helpful for you. Be open to constructive criticism when it comes to communication and behaviors. The same goes for the Avoidant and Anxious individuals. Allow people with good behavior patterns to teach you and show you the healthy way. You will read more about those healthy patterns throughout this book.

SUMMARY

If you recognize one of these patterns in your life, there are many other therapeutic methods to work on your attachment style and heal the core of the issues. We can fulfill some of our internal needs without help from our parents or guardians. You need to listen to what your inner Kid is telling you. Very often we need to build up enough functional behavioral strategies, healthy soothing mechanisms, and social support systems to bargain with your inner Kid. If you show yourself as a good role model and someone that can handle difficult situations, your inner Kindergarten of Parts will follow along and won't interfere as often. By Kindergarten I mean the complex system of your behavioral mechanisms and emotional reactions which are there to protect you and let you know that there is something bad going on.

Your inner Kids aka Parts will be actively letting you know that the situation isn't okay because you don't pay attention to them. If your Kindergarten is not nurtured, nourished, and appreciated you can't expect to have emotional balance and healthy relationships with others. To some it might seem trivial to keep on top of diet, exercising and being mindful and social. I can assure you it's not. If you don't have a healthy lifestyle the detrimental effects will be visible in your emotional regulation.

Having a good understanding of your attachment style is crucial for changing your dating and relationship patterns. You can address your issues only when you see them clearly and are courageous enough to acknowledge them and have the strength to change them. Your attachment pattern is an effect of upbringing, but I don't want you to blame the people who raised you. When you realize the origins of your behaviors it's much easier to change them, and your past actions start to make sense.

We are all sometimes jealous, insecure or avoid feelings. That's why I don't want to pathologize those feelings. But we need to work on them so that we can build healthy and stable relationships.

This chapter has examined all four attachment styles: Preoccupied, Avoidant, Secure and Fearful. I focused on advice and suggestions for the Preoccupied and Avoidant. I also added a word for the Fearful type of people. I have not explored Secure attachment style more because people with those patterns are very skilled when it comes to creating relationships; they are able to attach to others in a secure manner and don't get too anxious about relationships. We also discussed which styles mix and match well and which individuals should think twice before starting a relationship. The exercises and advice will serve you well on the journey of getting to know your attachment style.

Chapter 2:
Understanding Self-Esteem

A sense of internal worth is extremely important in all areas of life. It ensures that we make the best decisions for ourselves and gives us internal joy and fulfillment. If your self-esteem is at the right level, you can become a very skilled dater. While reading this chapter try to analyze the origin of your sense of self-worth. We'll focus on what is healthy when it comes to self-esteem and how to use guilt instead of shame to benefit your self-esteem, communication, and capacity to help others. Lastly, I'll give you some practical exercises.

There are different sources of self-esteem: external and internal. External self-esteem comes from owning assets, performing well in different areas of life, work or sports and opinions that others have about you (Real, 2018). Those things can certainly make us feel nicer about ourselves but if you are basing all your values on them, it will be hard for you to sustain your self-esteem and therefore feel good about yourself and others.

External self-esteem depends on external conditions, which as we know change often and cannot be controlled. As much as it's important to take others' opinions into consideration it's not functional to internalize everything that we hear. Also, if your assets and performance are not at your desired level, your self-esteem will lag or go up and down and that's not how you want it (Real, 2018).

Striving to be better is vital, we obviously want to be better than we were yesterday but comparing yourself to another person might not be very realistic as psychologist Jordan Peterson pointed out. Others have different upbringing, birth order, age, sex, race, economic situation, etc. Performance sometimes also changes across lifespan depending on which area of our lives we use to bolster our self-esteem. For example, we cannot have the same sports achievements at 25 and 80. You might also encounter difficult circumstances in life that stop you from performing socially, sexually, athletically, or professionally. Money also comes and goes very often.

Others can make us realize what could be possible and, instead of comparing yourself to them, use this realization to create goals based on the inspiration they have given you and your knowledge of a particular field. Then, create doable, timely and measurable steps to that goal and compare your performance from the beginning of that journey to what you have achieved so far. If you can see progress, that's amazing and you managed that without criticizing yourself and comparing yourself to others. Of course, if you believe that you can do things better and quicker, include those changes in the steps that you have created in the first place. One of the counselor's clichés is "don't focus on things that you can't control and pay attention to what you can."

Focusing on controllable things entails a level of interest in your career, assets and other's opinions but try not to see yourself as an extension of those things. What are controllable things? You can only control your behavior and even this has its limitations. You can't govern your emotions, thoughts, and external outcomes. You can take precautions and train your mind but there's no button that you can press. So, focus on your actions and mindset.

What is a more functional way to build up your internal self-worth? Internal self-esteem is much more reliable and is based on the idea that everyone as human beings is equal and not better or worse than anyone else (Real, 2018). If you believe yourself to be superior, then grandiosity can prevent you from making a genuine connection. On the other hand, if you think that you're worse than others, you will hurt yourself internally and prevent yourself from growing. Middle range is the healthy internal self-esteem, exactly where you want to be. Just like our parents loved us for being us, we can give the same to ourselves. Even if this was not the case in your household, it is never too late to reparent yourself and assume this type of everlasting and constant self-esteem that cannot be taken away from you.

When I explain the concept of internal self-esteem to my clients who have strong inner critic Parts, meaning they tend to criticize themselves, they sometimes get defensive. That's because internal self-esteem only appears if we stop criticizing ourselves. They don't want to take on this mindset because they believe that if they don't criticize themselves, they'll stop progressing. For some people, self-deprecation is a mechanism for improvement. I hear comments like "Well, if I'm enough and I matter just because I'm a human, then I don't have to do anything at all!".

I don't believe we can just sit back, look pretty, and do nothing that matters. The concept of internal self-worth shouldn't be your excuse for bad behavior either. Your situation, words and actions need to be acknowledged and improved as you go. We need healthy levels of guilt to let us know that we made mistakes, but not so much guilt that it turns into shame. Guilt is a feeling that lets us know that we performed a wrong or bad action and that we need to improve. Shame, on the other hand, is an overwhelming feeling that we're worthless as a person because of something that we did or because something happened to us or because of us. If you exchange shame with guilt, you create a healthy mechanism of growth and self-forgiveness and you heighten self-esteem (Real, 2018). This in turn helps you in life and in dating. To let you understand the difference between guilt and shame, here's an example of each emotion:

Shame: "I'm so stupid, why did I say it on a first date?! Of course, he won't respond to my text."

Guilt: "That thing I've said to him was a bit silly, but I was nervous, it happens. I hope he didn't get offended and will text me back. I'll try to do better on the next date."

Shame entails that you're intrinsically bad and it's impossible to change it. Guilt allows for improvement and realistic thinking. It also prevents deep internal damage that we do to ourselves by adopting a "shame mindset". Shame is also self-centering; it often prevents us from thinking of others and doing right by them because we're so wrapped up in feeling sorry for ourselves. Therefore, guilt can improve your capacity for good communication and helping others because you will be more emotionally regulated, realistic and solution focused. Shame dysregulates us very strongly because it brings in the notion that we're bad, can never change and therefore will never find happiness and fulfillment. Guilt, on the other hand, says, "I've made a mistake, but I can fix it or change it in the future". In shame we attack our own character and in guilt we disapprove of the behavior.

Good self-esteem and solution-focused thinking are very important in the context of dating. Shame is depleting and will lead you to dating burnout very quickly. Changing shame to guilt, using your internally created self-esteem to mitigate emotional turmoil, and treating failures like lessons will get you far, not only in dating but in life in general because you're building resilience.

I want to propose to you the concept of affirmations, they are affirming sentences that you repeat to yourself. Think of it as advertising to your brain, the more you advertise and the more you show people a product the more opportunity you create for selling it. By repeating a certain idea in your mind, you create an opportunity for it to be included in the most accessible part of the mind because you heard it recently. It's an extension of the idea "fake it until you make it". Research has shown that affirmations work well for increasing self-esteem and having a better body image (Armitage, 2011; Lannin et al., 2021). They also proved to be good for increasing self-efficacy, stress reduction and behavioral change (Charlson, 2013). Repetition works well with our minds and is good for creating habits and routines.

A lot of our important behavioral patterns that you want to change with affirmations come from your childhood. Every counselor will explore patterns from your childhood because during early age the brain is very malleable, and it's prone to automatize behavioral patterns that we learn from parents. In a way we're programmed by our parents, peers, and teachers through repetition. It's an innate mechanism that helps our species survive. If you learn useful skills early on and make them automatic, you're more likely to survive.

We are susceptible not only to useful skills but also to dysfunctional patterns of behaviors and if your parents had poor self-esteem for example, you are also likely to have it or to be the polar opposite. Perhaps you learnt that it's easy to manipulate or treat people with low self-esteem badly and that can lead to grandiosity. So, your care takers were affirming certain behaviors and installing them in you. This can be undone by affirming new patterns by yourself.

What people often don't realize is that we can also program ourselves in the way that we want. We can mindfully choose to go different ways but to do it we need to acknowledge our patterns and come up with functional ones that could be a substitute. It's not easy! There is no mom or dad or a guardian to install this in you anymore. So, you need to become this Functional Adult for yourself. When you repeat a thought or a behavior it can become habitual and later even automatic. We can create new pathways in your brain (Kays et al., 2012). Sorry defeatists!

Your affirmation could look like "I am a worthy partner" or "I practice my social skills regularly". You might say "But what I wrote in the affirmations is not true!". It might seem fake if it's not the way you feel or not something that you do just yet. Affirmations put your mind in a place where the achievement, situation, mindset are already there with you. And that can help you to stay on track and believe that the goal is achievable, that you are worthy of success, love, etc. It's like the Pygmalion Effect, when you remove the negative expectations, set the right but high expectations, train the person, and give them feedback and praise them for the success and you are getting yourself a great student (Boser et al., 2014). To apply this to inner work you need to be both trainer and trainee, you need to treat yourself and train yourself in a way that you can call yourself a good and happy human being.

Perform the exercises below to bring some healthy self-esteem to your life. I encourage you to start a therapeutic diary not only to perform the tasks from the book but also to note your internal experiences, thoughts, and emotions connected to those exercises.

* * *

INCREASING SELF-ESTEEM EXERCISES

1. AFFIRMATIONS

Did I convince you to start your daily affirmations? Great, let's go! Set yourself up for at least 5-10 different affirmations. But first think of your values and goals in life because they will help you form affirmations. Answer these questions to establish your values and goals:
- What do you value in life?
- What type of person do you want to be?
- What type of dater do you want to be?
- What type of a future relationship do you want?
- What are your other goals or values?

When you answer these questions ask yourself:

Are your values and goals healthy and realistic?

Will I be harming myself or others in any way if I think like this?

For example, if your attitude and goal is to be a person who doesn't "catch feelings" at all, which means to not to get emotionally involved with romantic partners. It means that your goal is out of balance. It's very common to go too far in the opposite direction if you were hurt many times because you got attached too quickly or to the wrong person. I have heard this countless times from people who care very much about the outcome of dates and have a Preoccupied attachment style. It's not human to not care at all, we're not robots, and you can't just push the "no feelings" button.

Try setting a goal like: "I want to be the type of dater who can enjoy the current date without getting ahead of myself and setting unrealistic expectations for this experience or for myself. I want to be mindfully present, enjoy my time and get to know my date better before planning for the future." This type of a goal is doable, healthy and gives your positive emotions and excitement an outlet. It allows for objectivity, enjoyment, and healthy boundaries instead of barriers. While writing down your goals try to keep this type of balance. For example, your goals can be to improve communication, be calmer, more confident, or funnier.

Your affirmations should be written in the present tense. I know it's tempting to add your typical "I will", "maybe", "probably", "at some point." Mindfully stop yourself! Think "I'm there! I'm doing it!"

Some affirmation ideas:
- I'm present during dates and enjoying the here and now.
- I listen to my date mindfully and with my undivided attention.
- I'm not setting unrealistic expectations for my date or myself.
- I'm enough.
- I'm lovable and deserving of connection.
- I'm beautiful inside and outside.
- I'm relaxed during dates.
- I'm my best self on dates.
- I put my best foot forward when I meet my dates.
- I enjoy dating.
- I like to meet new people.
- I'm a good person.
- I'm fun to be around.
- I'm smart and good at conversations.
- I deserve a great date.

You can pick from those, but I encourage you to create your own affirmations and not only the ones that refer to dating. You can create affirmations related to career, wealth, lifestyle, or your life goals. Make a commitment to do your affirmations daily and in front of a mirror to reinforce the effects with visual stimuli (Hay, 2016). Say it and mean it! It can be a great self-esteem booster when you make an effort to improve in different areas of your life.

2. ANCHORING A POSITIVE EVENT

Do you know those times when we feel really nice, positive and good about ourselves? When was the last time you felt like this? At a nice family event, maybe graduation, traveling or playing with your dog? We call those positive sensations in IFS therapy Self Energy and in RLT it could correspond with Functional Adult state. At these times it's so much easier to handle difficult situations, and to be understanding, curious and compassionate. You're probably thinking "I can't just have a great day every day! Impossible to have the same conditions for it!".

This is true but we can anchor feelings, which means remembering them in a somatic sense. Having this skill can help you snap out of what we call in IFS – blending with Parts and in RLT – Adaptive Child state. Snapping out of those states means to switch from your "reptilian brain" to your "human brain." Also, it indicates that you mentally changed from the Kid to the Adult state (Real, 2018).

To practice the explained above skills of anchoring, close your eyes, and position yourself in the situation where you feel those positive feelings like courage, curiosity, and calmness. Not only remember the events but try to feel with all the senses. Ask yourself these questions to increase your sense of these positive sensations:

- Where are you?
- What can you see?
- What can you feel on your skin?
- What can you hear?
- What can you smell?
- What can you taste?

Now ask yourself where is the positive sensation in your body? It can manifest in many ways, people talk about waves of sensations, images popping up or a particular body part that feels different. Now that you feel it, try to "anchor it", meaning to remember it and preserve it. This will keep you steady in the calmness like the ship anchor holds a boat during the storm. You can try dispersing the feeling around your body so that all parts of you can feel the positivity, you can even imagine it enclosing your body and breathing it in. Now you can use this skill any time you want, even with your eyes open.

Feeling insecure on a date? Getting nervous? Are you talking about something touchy and uncomfortable, and you can sense your body flaring up in different places? Perfect time to anchor the positive. You will think more clearly, be more coherent, less stressed, and more confident.

3. KNOW YOUR STRENGTHS

When a date isn't going great or if you're feeling insecure, it's easy to forget who you really are and what makes you awesome. In difficult situations we slip back into the Kid mode and self-deprecation kicks in. Sound familiar?

By nature, kids are self-centered and when something goes wrong, they might blame themselves. We lose our broad perspective and ignore any other possible causes. Mindfully stop! Go back to what you know about yourself outside of this situation.

EXERCISE:

Choose three qualities that you believe you have and write down three examples for each of them where you describe how you used this quality to your advantage.

Remember these qualities for the future and when you're faced with a tough situation, remind yourself that you are not the loser that you think you are. You have qualities, values and worth. Use them!

4. PORTRAIT EXERCISE

The first version of this exercise was proposed by Paul Roland (2005). I've adapted and expanded it to provide you with additional insights about yourself. Imagine that you're hosting an exhibition and one of the pieces is a portrait of you. You have commissioned an artist to paint you exactly the way you want to be painted. All your friends and family are coming to the opening night. With your words or artistic supplies show how this portrait would look like. You can even think of a specific artist or a style that you would like the artist to use. What colors are you using and why? What types of emotions are you conveying through structure, expressions on your face, and colors?

Now that you have an image in mind, imagine that it's the opening night! There will be three speakers going on stage during the event. You need to choose them from your relatives and friends. The speakers will be talking about your good qualities and examples of those qualities. Remember that there is no negativity allowed. Your family and friends are here to support you.

Who did you pick?

Now write down what each person would say about you.

How do you feel during the speeches?

What are the emotions, thoughts and memories that pop up?

Now imagine that there are no people there with you. The portrait was just for your private collection all along.

Would you change anything in the portrait and why?

Would you invite anyone to see your private collection?

This is one of my favorite exercises, which often catches people off guard. They show their true self while performing it. It can be very confronting so if this exercise seems too difficult or triggering, please try it at a different time. I sometimes have to repeat it a couple of times with people so that they feel comfortable performing it. It can reinforce the previous exercise "Know Your Strengths" and make you realize your good qualities and also show you how much you're willing to reveal to others and at what stage of your relationship.

＊＊

DECREASING GRANDIOSITY EXERCISES

We have spent most of this chapter talking about feeling better about oneself. But what happens when we feel so good about ourselves, we become grandiose? It can lead to disregard for others and unattainable expectations when it comes to prospective partners. That decreases your chance for a good and loving relationship, especially because you are blocking the love that is inside of you from coming out. Grandiosity is paradoxically also a sign of low self-esteem. We develop this mechanism of skewed perception of self to protect those low self-worth feelings and cover them up with fake confidence. As an only child, I admit I have been there and that definitely blocked me from feeling truly good and connected with myself and others. If you meet someone "confident" but unkind, you can be sure it's a mask.

1. GRANDIOSITY SELF-ASSESSMENT
Answer these questions to find out if you have issues with grandiosity:
- In the past, did you notice that you adore your partner at the beginning of the relationship, but you get bored easily and start looking down on your partner?
- Do you find yourself annoyed by people's small imperfections?
- Do you easily disregard others and their opinions?
- Does it feel like people are just not worth your time and energy?
- Do you catch yourself despising others or being indifferent to your closest friends and family?

If you answered "yes" to any of those questions you could be at risk of having issues with narcissistic behaviors and thoughts.

2. WE ARE ALL EQUAL HERE
Very often we need a reality check. So, write down a list of what you expect from your prospective partner. Now while being as objective as you can, see if you're meeting these expectations as well. Ask two friends what they think of your point of view.

What came up during this exercise? Write down your thoughts, emotions and memories that popped up for you during this exercise. If you discover that grandiosity slips into your dating life, remember to give yourself frequent reality checks and bring yourself back down to the ground before you fly far away from all your relationship and dating prospects.

***

If you are thinking "What does she know about low self-esteem?" let me tell you about my journey with it. My first experience with low self-esteem was at school, where I was often bullied for being very thin and not having any curves as a woman "should have". People thought I was anorexic, but it was just the way puberty hit me. I was resentful towards boys that rejected me and when eventually puberty hit me "right" I started to go into grandiosity and lack of respect for my partner at the time. I acted poorly because I was too young to be in a serious relationship but also because I was hurting. Eventually I found inner peace and balance in my self-esteem and that led me to more respect towards myself and others. I started to expect the same from myself and I do from others.

SUMMARY

In this chapter we talked about toxic sources of self-esteem which come from fixation on assets, impeccable performance, and other people's opinions. We also discussed internal self-esteem which is essential for steady and healthy levels of self-worth. Differences between guilt and shame were explored to show how guilt is more functional and better for self-esteem levels and your capacity to help others. Lastly, I presented numerous exercises which can help you with building up your internal self-worth. I listed a couple of tasks to manage narcissistic thoughts and behaviors. Self-esteem needs to be balanced; you don't want to go too far into guilt that it becomes shame nor into grandiosity. Stay grounded!

Chapter 3:
Handle Rejections Like a Pro

In this chapter, we'll explore your behavioral and emotional patterns when it comes to being rejected. Are you more likely to blame yourself or blame your date for getting rejected? Self-esteem brings us two new concepts: internalization and externalization of events, thoughts, and emotions. Usually, people with low self-esteem will be the ones internalizing rejections. This means that we think so little of ourselves that everything needs to be our fault. On the other hand, people who have issues with grandiosity will be mostly externalizing rejections, which means that nothing is their fault, and it needs to be someone else's. Neither style is healthy so we will also discuss the best way to handle rejection.

A very common occurrence in dating is rejection. No one likes it, but we can't date in a healthy way if we can't handle it. To mitigate the blow that being rejected gives us, we like to either internalize or externalize.

I can't count how many times I heard "I must have done something wrong" when a friend didn't get a call back after a seemingly great date. The above example was an internalization of a rejection. Then I would usually ask my friend: "What did you do that was so horrible?" They usually respond with silence, or they describe an event or a sentence that wasn't very impactful. If internalization is what you do, ask yourself "Could there be any other explanation?".

People have many complex situations in their lives like resurfacing exes, family emergencies, other dates, poor mental health, and all the regular events that come with life. Why is it that people make it all about themselves? Because it hurts you and you're trying to make sense of the pain and to get better results in the future. Look past the pain and rejection and see things objectively.

If you've put your best self forward, enjoyed yourself and were respectful, that's all you can do. If your date doesn't want to pursue anything with you then perhaps this was not a good fit. And that's okay as well, because we won't like and desire everyone we meet and not everyone will like and desire us. Now you have time to acknowledge your feelings, recuperate and try again with joy and mindfulness. Internalization can either get us to overanalyze in pursuit of improving or to burnout and give up all together.

Externalization of rejection, on the other hand, is strongly connected to grandiosity. I have encountered people who didn't like their date but were outraged because they didn't get a call back. Did you ever think to yourself: "How dare he?! I was totally out of his league, and he didn't text me?" or "She must be kidding. She wasn't even that hot and now she is not responding?!" I've heard that all before, too, and maybe even thought it at some point. This type of thinking takes us away from action and bettering ourselves and lets us blame the world.

We can even do both of these things at the same time. For example: "I didn't even like him and he didn't call me back, what a punk. I must have done something horribly wrong if a guy like that is ignoring me." You may feel like you're better than someone else, so you're grandiose but would also internalize because supposedly you failed at dating. What a way to bring everyone down in one go!

We perform self-centered behaviors and have self-absorbed thoughts when we get rejected. To change this thought pattern, mindfully stop yourself. Think again if your train of thought is rational, kind and objective enough. To learn how to override your externalization and internalization, perform a Mindful Check-In.

Your body and mind are going through something difficult so be extra careful with yourself and intensify healthy habits. Calmly accept that for a time you might be more emotional and reactive or withdrawn. Just because you accept it doesn't mean you should do nothing. Remember to keep yourself busy with healthy things. After regaining control with the Mindful Check-In, use the Post Rejection Recuperation Plan to address your feelings and needs after getting rejected.

* * *

10 Step Post Rejection Recuperation Plan (works also for break-ups):
1) You might still be in your Kid mode, so start with acknowledging where (or when?) you internalize or externalize. Use the Mindful Check-In and Anchoring a Positive Event exercise.
1) Vent to your friends, family or a therapist about your feelings and thoughts. Keep acknowledging where you internalize or externalize. You can also journal about it.
1) If needed, allow yourself to grieve. It might have been a one-off date, but what we really lose are the dreams that we created of this person and of the future together. Give yourself time to wake up from that dream.
1) If you're still internalizing or externalizing, acknowledge it and override it with mindfulness. Just because you stopped yourself once doesn't mean that those states won't return in future.
1) Check-In with your body and mind regularly. Listen to what they need.
1) Keep your healthy habits in check: exercise, healthy diet, mindfulness, social support, rest, self-care, and reduce drinking and other drugs. These are all helpful for keeping good mental health.
1) Allow for some quality "me time"; do something nice and kind for yourself.
1) Focus on what's important in your life: friends, family, career, project, and travel.
1) Try alternative therapies like embodiment practices, dance therapy or art therapy. You can also study IFS and do it yourself. It helped me tremendously during my last breakup.

1) Revisit dating when your body and mind are connected and happy with the idea. Use your Mindful Check-In to find out if you're ready.

* * *

It's important to remember how common rejections are. Being persistent and resilient are great qualities that will help you to find the right partner, job and many other things. Apart from rejecting a fair amount of strange individuals, I've also rejected great guys. They were just not the right men for me when it comes to beliefs, sense of humor, path in life or chemistry. But I am certain that they will make amazing partners for other women. They've done absolutely nothing wrong. I have also been rejected a few times sometimes in a nasty way but I've learnt how not to take it personally. I've accepted that people may have multiple personal reasons for not wanting to see me again, even if I really was on my best behavior. And I know from personal experiences that nasty individuals often have some unhealed wounds.

One time stands out for me. I went out with a guy on around 3 dates. He introduced me to his family and acted like he really liked me, confided in me about his dad's passing and we seemed to have a lot in common. On our last date, however, he started laughing at my lack of fitness. Even challenged me quite a bit with exercises because we agreed on a PT session. I'm not sure about you but a high intensity training where I can't catch a breath and feel judged every step of the way is still not my ideal date even though I'm very fit now. Mind you, he was a personal trainer without a trace of fat and I was just beginning my fitness journey. He also asked me if I will split a fine if he gets one for illegal parking. After such treatment I wasn't keen on seeing him either way and I did send him a message calling him out on bad behavior. I never heard back from him. It hurt for a time even though he didn't present himself as a good person. I internalized his comments about my appearance and externalized by blaming and hating him. Eventually I accepted that this type of rumination will not help me get over the pain.

We can sometimes blame ourselves for things that objectively had no relevance. One friend of mine believed that a guy who she dated abruptly left her apartment after sex because she had too many crochets and yarn at home which she was showing him.

You can see how we loose common sense and ability to think critically and allow multiple versions of situations to come to our mind when we are falling in love. Account for this in your love life and question your point of view and choose a healthy mindset.

SUMMARY

In this chapter we identified internalization and externalization of rejections and how to avoid them. We discussed the best possible mindset to adopt after rejections, which is mindful and present attitude, grounding yourself and focusing on self-care. I also mentioned the importance of Mindful Check-Ins and staying centered when faced with rejection. I've provided you with a 10 Step Post Rejection Recuperation Plan that could help you when you have been rejected by a date or a partner. Those resources will aid you during difficult times of rejections and breakups.

Chapter 4:
Idealization and Dehumanization in Dating

Now grandiosity and insecurity have brought us to another two terms that are popping up in the contemporary dating world: idealization and dehumanization. If you're on a grandiose spectrum, you might be prone to dehumanize and disregard your dates and, if you find yourself more on the insecure side, you can idealize them. Neither is healthy, so let's find the balance. In this chapter we'll explore why idealizing and dehumanizing keeps you from finding a good, connected relationship. I'll also provide you with some tips on how to stop yourself from creating fairy tales and how to watch out for abusive partners who you might be idealizing. Lastly, we will delve into cures for dehumanization.

IDEALIZATION AND FAIRY TALES
If you find that you tend to "catch feelings" very quickly, you fantasize about the far future with a person that you barely know or haven't even met in real life, you are most likely far down the insecurity and idealization spectrum. You get deeply hurt because you want the connection so badly that you would settle for an imaginary tale. Infatuation is a potent drug; it makes us feel so amazing that we want more of it.

When you are in love, your Oxytocin, Dopamine, Norepinephrine and Endorphins are having a ball. So don't presume to think straight during the initial phase of dating. Our body doesn't want us to think logically because that would prevent us from having unprotected intercourse, babies and extending the human race. It's a very clever system and if we want to override it, we need to understand it. People who have Preoccupied attachment style and idealize their partners have more issues with those hormones, because they get attached more quickly. Whereas individuals who dehumanize protect themselves with emotional barriers or remain unemotional like narcissists.

Have you ever had an encounter with someone so attractive you couldn't think straight? That's it, your body tells you "Go procreate, your babies will have a perfect jawline!" Jokes aside, the body tells you something more like "Go procreate, this person is super symmetrical, healthy looking, has good genes so your offspring will have greater chances of survival."

We call it the Halo Effect which explains that we're far more likely to trust and like people who are attractive (Ramaker, 2020). You're genetically wired to idealize them to ensure your babies are healthy and the planet occupied by your family. It's all automatic but it often can be accounted for and overridden with mindfulness. It doesn't mean you'll stop producing all the happy hormones, but it means that you can adjust your behaviors and opinions accordingly.

IDEALISATION AND NARCISSISTIC ABUSE
People who tend to idealize their partners might also find themselves dating and getting into relationships with narcissistic types of individuals or abusers. This tendency can be very dangerous not only psychologically and emotionally but also physically, socially, and financially. Narcissists live in a fantasy land where they're on top of the world and there's no one there to match them so whatever they say is the last word. Some might not be bad people, but their skewed perception stops them from connecting to others properly.

By narcissists I do not mean only people with a diagnosed Narcissistic Disorder but individuals who possess more narcissistic traits than the general population. Very few narcissists seek treatment because it feels really good to feel superior. Genuinely believing that you're the best and others are beneath you can have a detrimental impact on your social connections and your family, but you might not find it alarming because there's a deep belief that they're inferior anyway. These people normally are self-centered, arrogant in thinking and behavior, lack empathy and consideration for others, and exhibit an excessive need for admiration.

In the context of dating, they might also want a life partner like any other person. Often, they'll be looking for "the one." The perfect partner for them, who will match them in every way. And at the beginning they might even love boom you and really enjoy your company so that you might not realize that you're dealing with a narcissistic type. But once they see any normal human imperfections in a partner, they go back to default mode. It's impossible to match the standard that is set by a narcissistic person. So, you'll save yourself a lot of time if you leave the scene as soon as you notice this pattern. If you tend to be very blinded by dates and seek attention even though you identified red flags, it could be a sign of love addiction (Melody et al., 1992) or codependency (Melody et al., 1989).

If you must bend over backwards for a person from the very beginning and you can already sense microaggressions and snarky comments. Run! You can sometimes install boundaries if you're not sure if the abuse is truly there. People who exhibit narcissistic traits very often are looking for easy prey, so they'll be quickly discouraged if you'll be true to yourself and your needs. If you stop idealizing them, you'll see their behavior for what it truly is – abuse.

Even I who usually would be slightly more on the grandiose spectrum have been guilty of idealizing others. I have dated a narcissist before, only for a month but I developed strong feelings for him. It was the worst "break up", and I put break up in quotation marks because we were never an official couple that I have ever faced. My theory is that abusive relationships may be the hardest to get over because they don't make sense to us. I was asking myself: "How could you be so stupid to give him the time of the day!?". I was in disbelief on how I could feel so strongly about someone that treats me and other people so badly. The thing about abusive and confusing events is that our survival mechanism doesn't like them and wants to immediately make sense of them so that we don't make a similar mistake. Unfortunately emotions are not logical that's why it can be very hard for us to create logic where there is none.

I experienced typical narcissistic moves from him: gaslighting, rude jokes, deliberately trying to make me feel jealous. When confronted he would just deflect, avoid or try to make me feel bad about approaching him. The beginning of the relation was of course amazing, and he would still be charming from time to time to keep me "hooked". We get very addicted to the swing of very high highs and very low lows when it comes to emotions. Especially when we are fuelled by the "new love happy hormones" such as Oxytocin. Unfortunately we were also working together so when I broke it off, he started bad mouthing me to other employees and trying to get me to quit. My Functional Adult could see him for what he was, but a Part of me was still in love with the idea of him. This inner conflict was killing me, eventually I accepted that we can have two very conflicting feelings at the same time, for example longing and hate for the same person. I felt guilty and I promised myself that I'll do better next time. What really helped was to forgive him and myself.

To have a better perspective and stop idealization it can be a good idea to create an abundance of options for yourself and explore them with equal attention. So, you can try to engage in dating multiple people at the same time while keeping a good work-life balance. Even though some studies have shown that the bigger the options pool the less likely we are to make a choice (Pronk & Denissen, 2019) it could also make you realize that you do not have to settle for whoever pays attention to you. If you attend each of your dates mindfully and with respect, there is no harm in expanding your horizons a little. Do some Mindful Check-Ins to keep on top of your fairy tale inclinations and idealizing and try the following exercise. It's an exercise that many therapists would use in their practice.

* * *

EXERCISE: Ideal Partner List
Get yourself into your Adult state and think about all the qualities that you would like in a partner. Keep it as realistic as possible. You can also divide them into things negotiable and non-negotiable.

After a new date comes along you can compare them to this list and see if you have been idealizing them when they haven't even hit the Pass score! Don't bring your list to the dates, do it in your own time.

It might sound like just ticking off boxes, but I think it should be used more as a wakeup call when you know you're easily blinded by looks and/or attention. Look at the actions of this person and pay attention to the way they make you feel instead of playing house in your head.

Qualities of a good partner: (ideas for your list)
- Consistent (people can be chaotic but still be consistent with their affection for you).
- Caring.
- Present (when you need them to be).
- Respectful.
- Reliable (some people can be unreliable with timing but will be emotionally there for you).
- A good person.
- Kind.
- Generous (doesn't have to be money related, people can be generous with their time, attention, or support).
- Willing to work on the relationship.

I believe those ideas should find their way to every non-negotiable list out there. It will ensure that you do not get into an abusive or toxic relationship. Make a note that you should be displaying all the qualities that you included on your list. If you request it, you should be able to reciprocate in a similar way.

***

DEHUMANIZING

The other side of the spectrum is where grandiosity lives. Especially in today's times of online dating and endless choices, we can get into rejection and dehumanization mode very quickly. Plenty of options means plenty of painful disappointments. To protect ourselves from such an amount of heartache we protect ourselves with barriers. One of them is the dehumanization of other people.

Today's Western dating culture is called a "hook up culture" where we degrade others with a term that recently emerged called "body count" which means people whom we slept with. And we're expected to be okay with it because, apparently, that's what the majority is doing. I do believe this is the era in which we're the most technologically connected but emotionally disconnected. "Catching feelings" is passé, out of date and weak.

But let's change the narrative. I believe this is the most cowardly we've ever been. Dehumanization can step in, for example, when people are so afraid to get hurt that they avoid feelings all together. There is no way to find anything meaningful while dehumanizing. How brave and strong one needs to be to put themselves out there with their feelings on a platter! I admire this type of courage that's mistaken for weakness when it's actually vulnerability. The Gottman Institute has found that people classified in their study as "Masters of Marriage", meaning they wear their heart on a sleeve and are not afraid to get hurt in the process, have the most fulfilling love life (Lusignan, 2021). Brene Brown calls this type of person wholehearted. I hope that you who picked this book are aspiring to this type of lifestyle because that's where this book wants to take you.

So please, treat people the same as you would like to be treated and don't degrade them to a number. If you're prone to dehumanization and only looking to fulfill your desires but want to change and find a meaningful connection with someone, start with your daily thoughts.

When you catch yourself mindlessly checking people out just to lust after them, stop and try to see that person as a human being with issues, family, likes and dislikes. I find it more common in men and that type of mindset can lead to an unhealthy relationship with sex and desire. Very often when I treat sexual addictions this theme comes up. People who watch a lot of porn and start to do so early in life can have a dysfunctional idea about women, men, sex, love, and connection because they all start to fall into the same box as lust.

When it comes to committed relationships it's hard for those people to stop lusting after others and that can develop into an addiction. Those behaviors can take you away from what really matters like connection in life, relationships and dating. So, if you're having similar issues, please, go back to the "We Are All Equal Here" exercise or do a Mindful Check-In.

When the veil of dehumanization falls, it can be confusing and even painful. It was your mechanism for a long time, so you need a healthy substitute. That's where you can incorporate different self-soothing techniques such as self-talk, meditation and mindfulness, physical exercise and the exercises included in this book. It's uncomfortable to be exposed without your protective mechanisms but it will bring you closer to the essence of being human and all the wonders that come with it.

To cherish this new way of approaching dating and life, try to decrease your pool of choices and focus your attention on dating one person at a time. Give it a real go! If it doesn't work out it's okay, recuperate and revisit dating when your body tells you it's safe again. Welcome to humanity.

Admittedly, lack of respect and looking down at others have slipped into my patterns in the past because of feelings such as disappointment, hurt and fear of vulnerability. I can assure you that it's much nicer when you develop courage and skills to be vulnerable and nice to people. Dating and life in general feels more fulfilling, true and meaningful because you can appreciate it for what it really is rather than the idea of it.

SUMMARY

This chapter explores how idealization and dehumanization can influence your dating life in a negative way. Idealization positions you as an inferior party who worships a person they barely know. Creating fairy tales about the future is very common when it comes to idealizing. Pretending and lying to yourself is a form of self-betrayal that will hurt you in the future. On the other hand, dehumanizing prevents you from creating a genuine connection and, eventually, a relationship. This chapter shows you how to keep the balance in your connection to others via practical exercises. Make sure to be mindful about the level of your connection and actions that are aligned with it when you are dating. I hope you've realized that idealization and dehumanization are games of pretending that help us ignore our underlying emotions and take you away from reality. If you face your emotions and fulfill the needs of your internal Parts, you can safely live in reality, make better choices and be more fulfilled.

Chapter 5:
Barriers, Boundaries and Boundarylessness

To be able to lead a healthy life, achieve success in your romantic life and become good at dating you will need boundaries. Boundaries are rules that we set within ourselves and with other people. With these directives, we're better able to set and achieve goals, keep ourselves accountable and show people how to treat us and be around us. You can think of it as your own set of legislations that you need to communicate to others and comply with. There are so many conflicting Parts within us that sometimes one of them might want to "break the law." Perhaps you're holding yourself accountable to study four times a week, but one day your procrastination Part is kicking in, so you feel like not following through with one of your commitments. We always need to remind ourselves about what's important for us and boundaries help with that. In this chapter we'll explore different types of boundaries and explain the difference between boundaries, barriers and being boundaryless. I'll also include exercises to help you build up healthy boundaries.

Boundaries and barriers are both protective mechanisms, but barriers remove the possibility for connection to your other emotions and to other people. When you put up a barrier you create disconnection, and you can't nurture a relationship while disconnected. Barriers, for example, are avoiding conversations, ignoring a person that you are speaking to, dissociating, sarcastic comments or aggression.

Boundaries, on the other hand, keep you safe emotionally and physically but allow you to keep the connection going. If you're within your boundaries, you're able to listen to others better, handle difficult situations and make better decisions. On the other hand, being boundaryless creates an unsafe environment when one or both partners are imposing on each other's personal and emotional space.

We all have some automatic stress responses like getting visibly angry at someone, yelling, withdrawing, or submitting. They are all Kid state responses and, if you put up your boundaries, it's much easier for you to switch to your Adult state. Boundaries allow for connected relationships and preservation of independence and at the same time. To properly comply with your boundaries and to hold others accountable, you need to practice them every day. We constantly need to define and redefine them depending on the situation, time, and the person whom we interact with.

I call an individual who doesn't have well defined boundaries boundaryless. It means that this person has neither a protective mechanism against actions of others nor the protection from their own Parts, emotions, and thoughts. Those individuals will be impeding on other people's boundaries and will be easily rattled emotionally. So, boundaries are the sweet spot between boundarylessness and barriers.

There are different kinds of boundaries. The ones that we create for other people and the ones that protect us from the inside. Now we'll go into their descriptions and later we'll see how to create them in our lives.

EXTERNAL BOUNDARIES

External boundaries are a set of rules that we create so that people know how they can or cannot behave around us. Also, what they can do for us, with us and to us. Those will include for example the types of jokes or conversations we find acceptable. They'll also be a directive factor in how we define our personal space. Some people would love more closeness on the first date, but others will keep away for at least three or four encounters. Some will be okay with having sex on a first date and others won't.

Very often I hear from couples that their partner "should know" how to be around them. When you're in a long-term relationship, the lines of your boundaries might get blurred. You need to reinforce, cherish, and adjust your boundaries every day and not only in the first few months or years of the relationship. The beauty of being a human is that we grow and learn every day, so our values, thoughts and behaviors need to develop with us. Make sure that you keep your partners up to date when it comes to those changes.

When we judge each other's characters, we look for consistencies in behaviors so that we can establish our date's character. In this way, we can figure out if we're compatible. If your boundaries are not in place or if you want to impress your date so much that you pretend to have some desirable trait that you don't really possess, it can bring a lot of confusion to the whole dynamic of the relationship. If I had a dime for every time someone told me "After a few weeks, I felt like I'm dating someone completely different!" I would be on my way to Honolulu on my private jet.

As much as all of us act our best, tell our best jokes, and keep the quirks and flaws for later, it still needs to be You at the core. If it's not, your date is having fun with some nonexistent version of you. So, you can potentially be wasting everyone's time, because at some point the act will need to stop and both of you might realize that you're incompatible. To avoid disappointment, even on your first date, start installing your boundaries with people and be very clear about them. Some people might not like your boundaries and may lose interest in you because of them; let them make that choice. People will respect you more if you properly show them how to treat you. The ones that are not fit for you will quickly fly away and you will have a clearer view of people that stay and want to continue connecting with you.

The desire to impress someone or to seem "cool" can be overwhelming. But if you're breaking or pushing your boundaries you can hurt yourself in the process and the burnout might catch up with you. It's not worth it in the long run! Listen to your body and make the right decisions for you. No one is worth compromising your values for. The right person for you will appreciate that you are true to yourself.

To visualize this I want to bring in another example from my current relationship. We were two months into the relation, we were not officially a couple just yet because we decided to wait until we met each other's social circles. For context, the courting was quite long because before we met my date at the time had over 3 weeks of holidays booked, so we had to keep in touch via texts. Perhaps also because of the lack of label factor I felt uneasy and a bit insecure when he was rejecting my invitations to events because of other plans that he made beforehand. His rejections were more frequent and he acknowledged that and asked me at some point how I feel about that. At first I said that I understand and it's no ones' fault. I had more social events happening at the time and he was quite busy with other commitments so there was truly no one to blame. Nevertheless, some voice in my head was telling me "he doesn't like you as much as you like him", even though I objectively knew that this wasn't true. Once again I decided to be straight up about it. I always tell couple's that I work with to bring solutions not problems to the discussion. Therefore I explained to him how this makes me feel and that I struggle to be myself around him if this is not addressed and I preceded with a potential solution. I asked him to reciprocate with another invitation after rejecting my offer and in that way I can see straight away that he wants to spend time with me at a another time. He was very appreciative of my openness.

Again I could have stayed "cool" and "unbothered" but that didn't make me happy and was interfering with the way I perceive myself and this relation and both being true to myself and having a healthy relationships are my values. Seeming "chilled" was not as appealing as upholding my values. Luckily his communication is also very good and we both appreciate that we can openly talk about things like this without escalation. You can see that before you form your boundaries you need to remind yourself about your values and analyze what Parts of you need help at a certain time.

* * *

EXERCISE: Understanding Your External Boundaries

Write down your first date boundaries. You can divide them into categories e.g.,

- Sexual (how far do you want to go sexually or romantically?)
- Physical (define your personal space)
- Conversational (which topics are okay with you and which ones are not?)
- Behavioral (what behavior you won't tolerate and what are your behavioral expectations?)

REFLECTION:

Your boundaries can vary depending on your mood, your date, and the particular situation. Remember to listen to yourself. You might have rigid personal space rules, but perhaps a person whom you've met makes you feel super safe, and your body just wants to be close to them. Let it. If you deny yourself some experiences just because you wrote down different rules in the journal, it might backfire as well. So, keep asking your gut what feels right.

* * *

INTERNAL BOUNDARIES:

This type of boundary protects us from the inside. Metaphorically, it's the way we raise our inner Kids. It's a set of rules that we want to abide by in our lives. For example, stopping ourselves from internalization and externalization can be a healthy internal mechanism that is an internal boundary. To create your internal and external boundaries properly, go back to the set of your goals and values that you created when you were writing down your affirmations. They will guide you towards the best ideas.

Going back to may last personal example, I have a boundary to not to be openly angry at people but rather, think things over in my mind and communicate my feelings and come up with possible solutions before I start the discussion.

An example of this type of boundary can be committing to not criticizing yourself or to say "sorry" to yourself if you do that mindlessly. Also, vouching that you will perceive others' statements as opinions rather than the absolute truths. Internal boundaries are best created by internal repetition and mindfulness. Another internal boundary is, for example, promising to compare yourself to the person that you were previously instead of comparing yourself to others and perceiving others' achievements as ideas for improvement. To practice how not to internalize other people's opinions, that is, acknowledging those opinions but not to making them a part of our own world view, perform the exercise below. This exercise was first explained to me by my supervisor Karen Triggs.

* * *

EXERCISE: Boundary Wall
You can actively protect yourself in a very diplomatic way, to successfully stop yourself from internalizing, externalizing, imposing your view on others and to prevent others from imposing their views on you.

Imagine a wall in front of you. It can be made from anything you want: cotton candy, flowers, brick, etc. It must have a window through which you can clearly see your counterpart. My favorite idea so far is a glass wall.

Now when your date or anyone else says something that upsets you, or you disagree with, or they try to impose something on you or "throw" something at you, this wall is your protection. Imagine that all their sentences are hitting the wall and bouncing off it. Or even that their words stick to the wall so that you can see and consider if you would like to make them your opinion. But they won't penetrate the wall to get to you. You can also remind your counterpart that this is their perspective, and you have a different one. This wall will also serve as a reminder not to impose things on the other person or not to say something rude or cruel. Practice putting up the boundary wall and have it ready when you know that you'll be stressed or if you're expecting a difficult topic to arise.

A boundary wall is not a complete barrier; you still need to actively listen and connect to the person in front of you. Just because someone stated their opinion doesn't mean that you should make it your own. Considering it, however, can offer you a different perspective. With this skill you can become a very flexible and skilled conversationalist. A decent debater can state their perspective, a great one can look and present from many different angles. You don't have to agree with everything that people say, in fact it might become mundane if no one has anything to add or no one is stirring the pot.

* * *

SUMMARY
This chapter gave you an explanation of differences between barriers, boundaries and boundarylessness. Boundaries are the sweet middle spot that neither keep you away from meaningful connection like barriers nor do they make you overbearing as when you have no boundaries at all. We also go into deeper division between external boundaries that we create for other people and internal boundaries that we create within ourselves. In addition, I included some practical exercises that will help you develop both types of boundaries. These sets of rules are very subjective, and we should create them with the use of introspection. If your life is unbalanced and unhealthy, and your emotional regulation is lacking it might be hard for you to understand what you truly need from others and yourself. So, make sure to start with the basics and you'll improve at this "boundary art."

Chapter 6:
Behavioral Mechanisms and Partner Choice Patterns as Childhood Influences

In this chapter we'll explore different mechanisms from your childhood that you might be using in your life currently such as: worrying excessively, people pleasing, criticizing yourself or pretending to be something that you're not. I'll present you with some practical exercises and tips that will help you be more mindful of your inner Parts. After discussing your behavioral patterns, we will delve into your pattern of choosing partners that are also closely connected to your upbringing. I'll also include some suggestions on how to restructure those patterns.

Childhood is more influential than we care to admit. It's not only about sad and happy memories but also about what kinds of patterns were created in our lives because of those experiences. These patterns accompany us on our dates and later in relationships. They're right there with you when you're sipping Margheritas with the cute guy from Bumble, waiting for us to go emotionally deeper so that they can take over.

You might not realize that your micromanagement, perfectionism, inner critic, people pleasing and all other dysfunctional ways of being and coping are the residuals of what was modelled for you or what you had to cope with as a child.

To manage these behavioral mechanisms better, think of doable and quick activities that could alleviate emotions that you're facing in real time. Think of it as fulfilling the needs of the inner Kid. Ask with curiosity what is wrong and what can be done in the moment. Listen to your body and its reactions so that you can have a better understanding of what needs to be provided. This will position you back into your Adult state. You can even imagine that you're putting this Part behind you to protect it. This is a great visualization exercise that Terry Real from Relational Life Institute uses in his practice. I first heard of this technique during my RLT course. You can imagine this Part as a child, perhaps yourself at the age when you first used this Part of you.

This type of inner work can also help you understand how you feel about your date. Very often we're so blinded by excitement and raging hormones that we miss important cues and thoughts. So, make sure to do a few reality checks before, during and after dates. To understand your Parts better, perform the exercise below.

* * *

EXERCISE: Track Your Inner Mechanisms
In a journal, write down different mechanisms which you use on a regular basis. (Think: "How do I react or cope at my worst?")

Look again at the list that you've created and say hello to all your Parts. Now that you have met with your so-called behavior managers, keep tabs on them and think of healthier ways to perform their jobs and what's driving you to perform these behaviors. Managers like this usually cover up some difficult emotions that need to be locked away because of how intense they are. If you're able to stop managing behaviors and look those difficult emotions in the eye and soothe them, you won't need your dysfunctional mechanisms anymore.

This exercise is based on IFS Therapy. Some of your mechanisms might seem very functional and you might even love them because they helped you out through life. For example, your inner critic is often pushing you to achieve and do good at work or to have more motivation. You have never tried to be productive and motivated without it, so the prospect of not using this mechanism may seem scary for you. It's possible to be motivated, driven, and productive without beating yourself up. But it can be more difficult, it is also much healthier and will stop the criticism from leaking into your relationship and perhaps into a family later. It's a bigger chunk of work, but we should do it to achieve more fulfilling relationships. Working on these patterns allows you to foster better communication and a lower probability of dating burnout.

* * *

Inner work can be a long process but if you want to use some simple principles from the exercise above during your dates, it could increase your confidence and psychosocial skills. During dates but also outside of them you can keep monitoring what visitors are popping up in your mind, try to have a chat with them instead of only ignoring them or acting on these thoughts and feelings. Here are some examples of very common behavioral mechanisms and some practical ideas on how to alleviate the effects of those Parts on you.

* * *

EXAMPLE 1:
Feeling insecure or stressed? Ask yourself what exactly is making you feel that way. What can you do to make yourself feel more secure?
  Ideas on dates:
- Change tables if there's too much light or the music is too loud, and you don't know if your date can hear you properly.
- Go to the bathroom to take a breather and "regroup" in your head.
- Ask some questions so that the spotlight is on the other person and not on you if you need a moment to gather your thoughts.
- Mindfully switch topics if the current one doesn't suit you.

- Do a discrete mindful exercise like focusing on your breath for a moment, relaxing your muscles, pushing the air down your belly instead of lifting your chest while breathing.
- Remember your strengths.

* * *

EXAMPLE 2:

Feeling your people pleaser joining you?
    Ideas on dates:

- Be mindful of what you want and your reasons for responding in a certain way.
- Do a body scan, find where your People Pleaser comes up sensation wise. Be attentive when you feel a similar sensation coming in. Maybe it's time to speak out about something?
- Remember your boundaries and values and ask yourself if you've been following them.

* * *

EXAMPLE 3:

Is your inner critic third wheeling?
    Ideas on dates:

- Remind yourself to talk to yourself with kindness. If you forget, make sure to rephrase the Critic's words towards yourself.
- Remember your strengths.
- Remember your achievements in life. (You can even share them with your date if the conversation allows for it)

* * *

EXAMPLE 4:

Maybe there's a macho or an eager Part of you? The one that wants to impress or share something so much it sometimes goes too far.
    Ideas on dates:

- Just like with people pleaser, try to locate it in your body. What hap-

pens when you get the sudden urge to brag or interrupt your date? Watch out for this sensation. Maybe it's time to listen in and pay attention to the person in front of you.
- Allow your date to finish what he/she has to say. People like to be listened to with attention and enjoy it when we elaborate on their stories instead of abruptly changing topics.

* * *

The above suggestions can help you with your behavioral patterns. But we also have patterns in choosing specific types of partners. Have you ever heard the phrase "He married his mother" or "She has daddy issues"? It's a very common occurrence to pick a partner that is very similar to one of our parents. This phenomenon is called Repetition Compulsion. We're prone to seek assurance and nurturing from parents and, if some or none of those needs are met, we will still be prone to look towards their fulfillment. Because a life partner is the closest and most intimate companion for most people, we might be inclined to recreate the dynamic that we can remember from childhood to try and meet our needs in that way.

Of course, to some degree partners can be supportive and meet some of our needs. Nevertheless, partnership should have a balanced dynamic, whereas our parents or guardians, at least until we grow up, should not be our equals. A parent or a guardian chose to bring you into this world and/or look after you. Because of that, they also chose to meet your needs but did not require you to meet theirs. This dynamic allows a parent or a guardian a level of control over you so that they can raise you in safety and show you the way to live your life without their help later.

Sounds great but obviously it doesn't always work like that. Our parents were raising us with the tools they had at the time, with their own dysfunctional patterns of behavior and demons from their past. Often unknowingly they would show us how to treat partners or how to be treated in the future. I don't want to get you to just blame your parents. When you analyze those patterns and figure out how they came about, you now have a new task. Mindfully change them, so that you can spare the next generations and show them a functional and healthy way to be in a relationship and to choose a good partner. Perform the exercise below to find out what type of partner you normally chose.

* * *

EXERCISE: Blast from the Past
Think of your past partners, dates, situationships, or crushes. Pick three of them that you consider having had the most influence in your life. If you are ambitious, you can include everyone. Now, next to their names write down their most prominent qualities and flaws that you recognized. Next to each of them, write down what drew you to them. Compare them and see if there are similarities.

Now think if you can point to any similarities with your childhood role models or perhaps if there was a dynamic between you that mimicked patterns experienced in the past at home or with previous partners.

REFLECTION:
If you're mostly happy with your past choices and perhaps only waiting to find the right person for you, it might have been just a fun exercise to make you realize the power of the past. But if you're not content with the quality of your relationships so far and want to change the narrative, perhaps it's time to consider other types of candidates.

* * *

Now that you're aware of your partner choice patterns, I want to outline some examples for you. Perhaps you'll be able to find some useful tips for yourself. Bring your Adult mode online and consider if the examples resemble your partner choice pattern.

* * *

EXAMPLE 1:
If your "go to" partner is a "bad" or emotionally unavailable boy/girl that you will be desperately trying to change or save, here are some ideas for you:
- Create boundaries early on and stick to them. Leave when your date doesn't respect them.
- Put yourself first and make sure you're comfortable.
- Make sure you keep your "rescuer" Part at bay.
- Try dating people from a different "category". A good guy/girl can also surprise you and might be exciting and funny when you get to know them better. Give it a go for a few dates.

All you can do is show your date how you want to be treated and the consequences if they won't respect your boundaries. Stick to your word and follow through with what you say. I personally saw people change and grow up when they met someone that they genuinely loved and wanted to be with. I was convinced that people don't change and, therefore, it's better to move on if someone isn't suitable, I now understand it depends on the types of issues they have and how love can motivate them to overcome these issues. Nevertheless, dramatic changes are very rare.

But a true, healthy, and equal relationship will never happen in this way if your Part that wants to save your match manages your behaviors; you need to allow this type of a partner to come to you and change because they want to. And believe them if they say they're not ready for a relationship.

You might have been so wrapped up in falling in love with just one type of person that you didn't realize it's time to change the script. An archetype of a "bad" boy/girl is so mesmerizing not only because of childhood patterns but because often they also exhibit qualities that keep us entertained. A person who is securely attached and is a good partner can also have these qualities, but perhaps you have never paid much attention to them because they don't have the James Dean vibe or the certain type of reputation that's so appealing to you. Look beyond the societal archetype and your bias towards rebels without a cause. Give a "good" guy/girl a chance. They might surprise you in other aspects of life like an adventurous hobby, kinky bedroom personality or being an undiscovered stand-up comedian.

It would also be interesting for you to trace your rescuer Part back to your childhood. Perhaps you're choosing someone to fix because you couldn't fix one of your parents? Or maybe one of your parents had the rescuer Part as well but could never fix your other parent? Maybe your father or mother was this "bad boy/girl"? When you understand the history of this particular choice pattern, you are better able to go the other way.

* * *

EXAMPLE 2:
If you usually choose good but boring dates and believe that they just need to open up more and that you'll be the one to find their hidden personality, then here are some suggestions for you:
- If there's no way for you to adjust to who they truly are as a person, you will probably save both of you a heartache if you don't pursue them further.
- You could possibly tell them that personal growth is important to you and ask them to gain more knowledge on topics that interest you, so that you can have more things in common.

I'm truly unsure of how frequently this issue arises in others, but it's admittedly part of my own past. Unfortunately, temperament and level of complexity can't be changed, like attitude and behavioral patterns. You just might be barking up the wrong tree. If you crave excitement and fun, but all the suitable and appealing partners lack such qualities, you might need to look further for someone that will be the combination of security and adventure. A mix like this is not easy to find, but it's possible. To find what you're looking for, you need to exhibit it yourself to a certain degree because your desired rare mix will most likely be looking for a rare mix themselves. If you're a shy type wanting an exciting partner, you might need to work on your social skills. I was a shy type that just needed to go outside of her comfort zone and practice, practice, practice. When you overcome your fears, it's much easier to open up safely to others and show them the fun and exciting side of you. If, however, you're having difficulties with the "secure" side of the mix perhaps it's time to investigate your attachment style and do some inner work through introspection or therapy.

This type of partner choice is in some ways similar to the first one because it also indicates that you want to "fix" the person. Try to trace this pattern back to your childhood. Maybe your parents' marriage was boring and sexless but nice and you've always craved more excitement? Maybe you crave someone that respects you and is stable, but a lot of people like this will also be quite simple? If you're a complex individual, you will not find fulfillment in simplicity. I don't claim that simple or complex are bad or good. They both have pros and cons. I believe that we need to accept who we are and find a partner that will be suitable for our respective temperament and level of complexity. Believing that someone incompatible with us will eventually stand up to the task because you have great chemistry is a fairy tale.

I was usually opting for this type of guys because I couldn't stand cockiness or disrespect from men. There was no way that I would put up with someone that treats me badly. Then usually stable guys were not very complex. I knew that I was looking for someone who can talk to me about intellectual things, but also be silly with me and go out for a party. Someone that is also emotionally intelligent, ambitious and looks after himself. I wanted a full package, but I knew I can get one because I was quite versed in all those different areas. At some point I gave up and thought I will never find this person, until I did. Main advice is, if you want something you need to specify it, project the same to the word, be proactive and patient.

**

EXAMPLE 3:
If you choose abusive partners, these are ideas for you:
- Create boundaries early on and stick to them.
- Present partners with consequences if they don't respect your boundaries.

- Be mindful and observe their behaviors.
- Don't create fairytales about the future with your new dates, enjoy the present moment.
- If you see that abusive patterns are present and your date or a partner doesn't want to change them after you voice your needs and concerns, stop contacting them.
- Monitor your insecure Parts, they might be telling you to stay and endure bad treatment, you need to make them realize that you want to break the cycle for good.

If you've been in abusive relationships before, you need to pay extra attention to abusive cues. Very often victims of abusive relationships come from abusive families. What we experience as children influences our current life greatly. If you experienced abuse from your parents on a regular basis, you might be thinking that it's normal in relationships. It will be more difficult for you to distinguish good and bad behavioral patterns because there was no prominent positive influence in your life. If there was abuse in your past, it's very important that you educate yourself about abusive behaviors and learn new functional life strategies, for example in therapy.

In some cases also early romantic relationships can set you up to be prone to endure abuse. I heard from few different people that their family wasn't very abusive but their first partner's were. When you face abusive situations and stay in them for longer you develop coping mechanisms that allow you to continue in this horrible situation. I heard that people learn how to quickly please their partner, avoid particular topics or give in sexually to divert the abusers attention. Even though you are averting conflict now you are betraying yourself in the future. That's why timing is so crucial. The less time you give to the abuser the better.

***

EXAMPLE 4:
If you pick your best friends with whom you have no sexual connection, these are suggestions for you:
- Establish your sexual needs before you go into relationships.

- Make sure that your prospective partner is on the same page when it comes to sexual needs.

Some couples don't put much emphasis on sex, and they are happy with few sexual encounters. But if you have experienced lack of sexual fulfillment in a relationship in the past, it could be a sign you have not been on the same page with your partner in a sexual realm. If you're not asexual (not interested in having sex at all) and want to have a successful relationship, you need friendship and sexual attraction otherwise you might end up feeling like roommates instead of partners. Sexual interest and attraction can't be faked or created. If you, for example, do not like your partner's body and you need this physical attraction to create a sexual connection, then it might be difficult for you to be romantically and sexually interested in your partner. Physical attraction is unlikely to appear unless your partner changes the way their body looks, for example through exercising, a healthy diet and hygienic care and grooming. But if it's not possible, your mutual attraction won't just magically appear if it has never been present. Of course, if you're the type of person that needs to get to know your partner and fall for their character, this also counts as an attraction. If intellectual and emotional connection evokes your desire that's great! But if the sexual pull is absent, you have a problem.

Friendly connection is very appealing, we might want to preserve it and deepen it through going into a relationship with that person. But if you don't find your date erotic at all, it can lead to disappointments on both sides later on. Sex might not be a very important side of a relationship for you, but it might be for your partner so talking about it beforehand is a respectful and mindful thing to do. If you're asexual, you can of course still find a meaningful connection with someone that will be happy with lack of sexual contact, but make sure that you're up front about your preferences and don't force yourself to go against your nature.

Try to trace this pattern back to your childhood. Are you just not interested in sex? If so, explore the reason. Were there a lot of shameful messages about sex in your childhood? If so, perhaps you could pursue some sexual awakening and healing with a sex therapist who could help you discover how shame is affecting your libido and partner choices. Maybe there are other events or emotions that prevent you from being more sexual. Or maybe a Part of you thinks that you don't deserve a sexually and visually compatible partner? If so, you might have an Inner Critic Part that fears failure. Explore other possibilities as well.

I find that people with this inclinations are very practical and pragmatic about life in general. They pick their romantic match because it's "good choice" logically. The problem with this type of mindset is that we humans are emotional and desirous. Emotions are not logical, but we should account for them because they are a vital part of us. Look at relationships in a broader spectrum. We need to be objectively and practically compatible but if chemistry and sexual pull is not present then a big component of a healthy relationship is missing.

* * *

EXAMPLE 5:

If you choose partners that will be the carer for you so that you can cope with your life, here are some suggestions for you:

- It would be worth it to explore this issue with a therapist if your behavior is codependent.
- Create an appropriate distinction between your life and the life of others. Which is just another way for me to advocate for good boundaries and to not let other people's issues impact you if you are not at capacity to help.
- Try to live an independent life before you consider dating again. When you can comfortably look after yourself, then you can safely let another person into your life.

It's hard to admit codependency, but with the help of a professional you might find it easier to get your life in order. Perhaps you have always relied on your parents and switched from your childhood home to living together with your partner? Or you have been going from relationship to relationship without any time to enjoy single life?

Try to objectively answer the question: Can I survive and live a normal life without a partner? If your answer is "no", perhaps you're relying too much on other people. A partner can obviously enrich your life and make you happier, but they shouldn't be used as a servant.

Trace this partner choice pattern back to childhood. Maybe you had an overbearing helicopter parent who was doing everything for you and didn't let you make your own decisions? If so, now having an independent life as an adult may seem unfamiliar and scary so you try to find a partner who will also care and decide for you. With hard work and practicing decision making you can become more self-sufficient.

I find that people who have this issue often come from religious communities were it's not appropriate to leave out of a family house, let alone having a relationship without marriage. Of course you can choose your religious beliefs and practices as you please, but perhaps account for this factor if you are in a similar situation. You can live with your parents and still be very independent person. Nevertheless, it's just easier to rely on others an to get use to this state of things. Just because something is comfortable it doesn't mean that it's good for you or your relationships in a long run.

* * *

EXAMPLE 6:
If you date very submissive types of people and you've put yourself in a role of a carer and your relationships haven't been very fulfilling, here are some ideas for you:
- Even though you support someone, you can still be codependent. Perhaps it's time to explore this possibility with a trained counsellor.
- Establish your boundaries and implement them early on.
- Make a clear distinction between others' individual life problems and your personal commitments. Support those close to you where appropriate and when you don't feel that it burdens you and draws from your backup energy levels.

- Address your carer Part with a professional.

If this sounds like you, there is a likelihood that you have been a carer not only when it comes to romantic relationships. You might have been the responsible person in your childhood already. If from an early age you have been looking after your parents, your relationship dynamics can be easily affected. Kids who become independent quickly are very capable, but also tend to forget about their own needs. You might not be familiar with asking for support from your romantic partner and that can create imbalance in your relationship.

To address this problem, you need to use mindful recognition of submissive and codependent behaviors in yourself and other people. It might feel somewhat uncomfortable to not be constantly needed because that gives you more room for your difficult thoughts. Those emotions and voices have been most likely waiting for you to address them for a while. It might make you realize that your inner work has been lagging and that you need to put more emphasis on it.

If you are the only active party in your relationships you are not actually developing connection. For an equal and balanced partner connection reciprocation of some sort needs to be present. Where as with excessive helping behaviors you are preventing it from happening.

**

EXAMPLE 7:
If you have been inclined to date self-absorbed and avoidant individuals who are not that interested in you, those are some ideas for you:
- Write a list of your relationship needs.
- Assess if your needs are objectively appropriate and achievable. (Ask for opinions)
- Implement your boundaries and state your needs clearly as soon as it's timely acceptable and reasonable.
- Search for a partner that has secure or slightly preoccupied attachment style.

- Stop chasing them!
- Assess objectively through conversations with them if they are truly interested in seeing you.
- Pay attention to the rates of your respective investment in your relation.
- If you need more investment, request it, and accept defeat, and walk away if your date doesn't want to invest in you.

If you find that you need more attention from your partner who is Avoidant, and you're more on the Preoccupied spectrum, it could be the time to fortify your boundaries and state your needs. Nevertheless, you want your needs to be presented in a timely manner and appropriately to the level of commitment in your relationship at the time. If you just had the first date with a person, you can't ask for immediate displays of affection and proclamations of love. But perhaps you can ask for a reassuring message after the date if your match is still interested in seeing you again. If your potential partner isn't willing to fulfil any of your needs for closeness and they're not up for negotiating alternatives and/or make fun of you for having such needs, they might not be the best pick for you.

Not only Preoccupied individuals pick Avoidants, but these two types are prone to seek each other out (Melody et al., 1992), especially if both had very dysfunctional family dynamics. If your environment as a child was unpredictable, you learn that you have to be needy and call for attention that you lack (Melody et al., 1992). Then Repetition Compulsion is doing the rest of the work. So, you're compelled to seek out similar distant and unpredictable dynamics in your romantic relationship. It seems familiar to be with someone that doesn't give you enough attention. If you find yourself in this description, it's best if you stay away from the Avoidants. What you need is closeness and security. I do believe trauma and unhealthy attachment patterns can be remedied with the right type of relationship. If your significant other makes you feel safe and gives you closeness, you might feel fulfilled enough to start addressing deeper issues from your childhood.

***

EXAMPLE 8:
If you are choosing the hottest people in the room but it never goes anywhere, these are the suggestions for you:
- Try lowering your appearance standards and focus on finding out what could attract you in someone's personality. Pick someone that you still consider physically attractive and give it a true go.
- Put more effort into your body, clothes, and general appearance.
- Put more effort into developing your social skills.
- Put more effort into other areas of your life such as career, wealth, personal development and gaining new knowledge.

Even though I have focused mainly on emotional and behavioral aspects of dating, we can't forget how visual we are. The brain is our greatest sex organ but our occipital lobe, which makes sense of things that we see, is a big part of it. The truth is we mostly date within certain appearance standards whether we like it or not because everyone else is doing it. Some people will be paying all the attention to their date's character but most of us will also be thinking about the way our date looks. This comes from the evolutionary and reproductive features of humankind. The more attractive the partner, seemingly the better the genes and the more likelihood that your family will survive. But to date in the higher attractiveness bracket we need to bring something to the table such as a similar level of attractiveness or other appealing traits. Currently there is a strong emphasis on promoting inner beauty and that is truly wonderful.

Nevertheless, we are not blind to other people's physical features, and obesity doesn't just become healthy and appealing. Admittedly my guilty pleasure is social media and there I see many videos made by girls that were rejected by men when they were bigger. They started going to the gym, got very fit and bragged about rejecting the guy who didn't want them in the first place. I do not believe that the moral from those stories is "horrible man rejected a great girl and now he got what he deserved". I believe the lesson to take way from this is: "when you get fit and healthy, more people are interested in you." You show others that you look after yourself, are motivated and passionate about it and your body looks amazing.

I went through a similar journey, I decided to get fit and eat healthy and lost over 15 kilos, my skin, hair, and the rest of the body looks and feels way better. I definitely feel more interest from men. I don't blame all the men that didn't want to date me in the past, as I also rejected people because I didn't find them physically appealing. This transformation definitely made it way easier to attract my ex and my current partner. I think we all should do it because that way you honor your body. In saying that, I don't mean that you should go on unrealistic diet or kill yourself in the gym every day to the point of depression. It took me over six months to get into shape but I'm still on a journey to perfect what and how I eat and my training schedule and I'm having fun with it. It is also amazing for my mental health and emotional regulation. I would never want to go back to my past state now, because I feel too good.

Apart from looking after your appearance, you can also attract people in the higher appearance bracket if you develop in other areas of life like career, social skills, or hobbies. If you are successful, funny and have exciting interests, people naturally gravitate towards you. In my opinion especially if a man is not very attractive, developing those aspects can make him very appealing. I find that women can overlook the appearance more than men can. Women are sometimes more focused on characteristics like being ambitious, funny and a good partner. Whereas in my view, men are looking for an attractive partner as it's a sign of status in some male circles.

Being the best version of yourself is a big chunk of what you can do if you want to date highly attractive people. Nevertheless, it is important to start choosing partners that are truly interested in you. If you are chasing people who don't want you, you are setting yourself up for failure. And even if we get the most attractive person in the room, they might not be the most compatible for us.

Trace this partner choice pattern to your childhood. Perhaps one or both of your parents put a lot of emphasis on physical looks? If they have been programming this type of thinking in you, then you might get an idea that this is the true denominator of a relationship. It can be difficult to lower your appearance standards but it's not impossible. Get to know your dates better, make sure to go on a few dates instead of just one. Sometimes we might start lusting after a person just because they've been around us a lot and we like their presence even though we weren't attracted to them on the day we met them.

SUMMARY

This chapter talks about childhood influences such as our automatic behavioral mechanisms and partner choice patterns. We talked about managing and changing your subconscious mechanisms such as inner criticism and people pleasing. Please, remember that those are just the most common examples of Parts, so you constantly need to keep a look out on what Part is coming in to guide your behaviors and thoughts. I hope that the exercise provided will help you to recognize and bargain with your behavioral mechanisms. I also outlined how the parenting style that we experienced as kids has an influence on our current partner choices. I gave you some examples to help you realize what your pattern is so that you can make sense of how it came about and how to change it.

Chapter 7: Crash Communication Course

Good and effective communication is one of the most important skills that you will ever learn in life. It can help not only your career, but also in finding and maintaining personal and romantic relationships. If you have other skills and values that you want to bring to the table, they will not be visible and appreciated by others if you cannot communicate them. This chapter will explore what a good communicator is. I will also provide some practical tips on how to communicate effectively. Next, I'll provide an exercise to help you identify your dysfunctional patterns of communication and give you some ideas for changing them. During those exercises you'll be able to reflect on your communication style and contemplate where it came from and how to fix it.

A good communicator is composed and has great emotional control. If you're able to distinguish different Parts of you that have opposing opinions, or the ones that are trying to sabotage you, you can negotiate and build trust within yourself. If you can be a good inner communicator and have a peaceful, disciplined mind you can become truly masterful when it comes to emotional regulation. If you can make sense of all the voices in your head and recognize your inner Adult voice and use it, you are well ahead of others.

Further skills you can build up on top of your emotional and body regulation. The next step is to forsake the ego, judgement, and notion of a black and white world. To be truly amazing at conversation, we need to allow others to have their say on their perspectives, and opinions. If we don't, we might as well stay home and perform a monologue.

When you're communicating, try not to speak in absolute terms like "always" or "never", especially when you're presenting an opinion about someone else. Give your counterpart space for adding their input, for example by saying "in my view...". As long as people are not rude or inappropriate, we need to respect their statements. You don't need to agree with everything people say, but you need to show some respect for the person and the interpersonal exchange. If you do get emotional during a difficult conversation, talk about your emotions instead of from emotions. I first learned about this concept during my RLT training. Here are some examples for you to understand the difference between speaking from and about emotions.

Talking from the emotion looks like: "You inconsiderate little man! Forgetting our anniversary!? I bet you wouldn't forget if it was a football match!" (Screaming and gesturing in anger).

Talking about emotions looks like: "Honey, I'm very angry about what happened yesterday, I felt alone and sad because you forgot about our anniversary."

Who would you respect more? A person throwing a tantrum or a person with a dead serious gaze talking about their profound inner experience. The latter is definitely more captivating and bearable. If you clear your mind with inner work and if you practice your composure while discussing tough subjects, you can become a formidable communicator.

Talking from your emotions is one of the dysfunctional patterns of communication. To manage your toxic communication patterns, remember to talk about people's behaviors that trigger you and your emotions towards them, and make a specific request to ensure the behavior and the feeling doesn't appear in this way again. You also need to remember that people don't have to grant your requests but if they would like to stay in your inner circle, they need to negotiate with you. If they don't want to resolve the issue, it means that the connection between you decreases. If someone promises change but doesn't deliver, you need to come up with consequences for their behavior and inform them about those before you implement them. For example, your consequence can be withdrawing your support, help, or company.

To manage your emotions, you can also use a Time-Out procedure invented by Terry Real (10 Commandments of Time Outs in a Relationship, 2023). This procedure was created to give you space to calm down and to give you the time to get yourself into Adult state and to prevent giving the cold shoulder to your counterpart. You must inform your counterpart that you'll take a Time-Out to cool down and let them know when you'll return. Don't let anyone physically or emotionally block your way; it's abusive behavior. Use Time-Out to calm your body, not to ruminate over the situation or what you'll say when you come back. Terry Real also suggests avoiding the issue straight after the Time-Out and waiting to adjust to the company of your counterpart again before reengaging. To move away from your toxic communication pattern, this exercise below is helpful. The exercise that follows will explore specific communication problems and provide several remedies.

* * *

EXERCISE: STOPP (STOPP Technique — ANJ Counselling & Psychotherapy, n.d.)
This exercise will help you catch yourself before your dysfunctional mechanism takes over. It's called a STOPP exercise. This lovely exercise is often used by therapists to treat anxiety, but I wanted to show you how to use it in the context of communication. STOPP stands for:

S – Stop
The first letter stands for 'Stop!'. It means that you need to learn to acknowledge that you're overwhelmed by emotions such as anger or that you're stressed and stop whatever you are saying or doing. When you're overwhelmed or angry this might not be the best time to state your opinion or act. If the situation does not permit you to stop, try to focus on one object in the room and bring yourself back to a balanced state or focus on your breath.

T – Take a breath
Your breathing pattern is closely connected to your emotional state. If you're stressed, you're likely to take shorter and more rapid breaths because you're not getting enough air. When we're stressed, our bodies can go into a "Fight, Flight, Freeze, Fawn or Submit" response. This response comes from our "reptilian" part of the mind; the part that relies on instincts to avoid getting hurt.

Our ancestors were running from tigers, but our opponent can be even more dangerous because we don't always see them: meetings, phone calls, emails, obligations. We cannot run from them, literally fight them, or just freeze and hope they'll disappear. But those stressors create the same automatic response. Our logically thinking brain cannot make out what should be done to avoid the stress, so the tension piles up in our bodies and comes out as sweating, trembling, headaches, numbness, dissociation, even red spots on our bodies. Anxiety manifests differently for everyone but it prepares us for escape.

That is why it is so important to focus on your breath and try to normalize it. Take a few deep breaths or hold your breath for 8-10 seconds. This will let your body know that it is not in any danger. This way we can override our automatic response.

O – Observe
Do a reality check. Ask yourself questions like:
Where am I?
How serious is the situation?
What am I thinking and feeling?
What is my mind saying?
Is this fact or opinion? Description or evaluation? Accurate or inaccurate? Helpful or unhelpful?
What unhelpful thinking habit am I using (e.g., trying to guess what people think, thinking the worst…)?
Where is my focus of attention?

P – Pull back / Put things in perspective
See the situation as an outside observer. Ask yourself questions like:
What would someone else see and make of it?
What advice would I give to someone else?
How important is it right now, and will it be important in six months?
Is my reaction proportionate to the actual event?

P – Practice what works
Do what works and what's most helpful. Use your values to determine what should be your course of action. Ask yourself questions like:
Will it be effective and appropriate?
Is it in proportion to the event?
Is it in line with my values and principles?
What will be the consequences of my actions?
What is best for me and most helpful for this situation?

* * *

I encourage you to start researching functional communication strategies and treating communication like a subject that should have been included at school. Perhaps no one taught you about communicating, but as an adult you need to teach yourself things that the system won't show you like paying taxes and running your own company. The exercise below will outline dysfunctional communication strategies so that you can determine which ones you might be using. Apart from examples of those strategies, I'll also include some specific remedies that you can use to stop those bad mechanisms.

* * *

EXERCISE: Fix Your Dysfunctional Communication
I would like to give you some examples of dysfunctional communication. Before reading them think about what you do during difficult

conversations or arguments. Below every dysfunctional communication style, I'll include some remedies and tips. To fix your personal communication impairments you need to identify what you do wrong. So, think about what you do at your absolute worst when it comes to interactions with others.

☞ Withdrawal

Withdrawal usually appears because people are too stressed about the interaction at hand. So, soothing techniques like deep breathing, mindfulness or meditation can be very effective. Others may withdraw in superiority to punish their counterpart. We often call it silent treatment or a cold shoulder. When you do that acknowledge that there are some difficult emotions inside of you like anger, resentment, or the need to "get even". Stop yourself and get yourself into your Adult state with relaxation techniques and/or exercises available in this book for example, "Anchoring a Positive Event". When you calm stress, anger, and all other Parts you need to go back to your counterpart and try to resolve the issue again with courage. You can also use the Time-Out.

☞ Yelling

Often people would resort to yelling because they don't feel heard. The problem is that when you start yelling, people listen to you even less at times because they're in a defensive mode. Instead talk about your emotions and come up with requests and consequences if someone is not holding up their end of the bargain and overpromising. When you feel the need to yell, acknowledge it and perform the STOPP exercise or a Time-Out.

☞ Putting people down/blaming.

Blaming will get you nowhere when it comes to problem resolution. Instead of pointing a finger at your counterpart, point it at your emotions. Don't attack people's character, but rather talk about what they could change in their behaviors to avoid hurting your feelings. Try to assume partial responsibility for some things. Perhaps you've escalated the conflict in some way? Acknowledge when you start blaming, perform a STOPP exercise, or take a Time-Out.

☞ Defensiveness.
Acknowledge when you get defensive and choose to see your involvement in the issue. Take on at least a tiny fraction of responsibility and focus on a solution instead of escaping from responsibility. If you know that you often get defensive try to acknowledge it before it happens, perform a STOPP exercise, or take a Time-Out.

☞ Complaining.
No one likes nagging, so make requests instead and make them as specific as possible. If it's more connection that you crave, talk about what connection is for you and what types of specific behaviors would make you feel connected. Explain why this is so important to you. If someone promised to fulfill your request and didn't deliver, then you need to come up with appropriate consequences. Empty promises can easily disconnect you further, so you can protect yourself by removing your support towards that person or by not granting them the pleasure of your company. Eventually, your last resort is leaving the relationship. There's no point hanging around if there's no connection left.

☞ Sarcasm and ridiculing others.
Sarcasm and laughing at others are a sign of growing contempt, and feeling contempt for another person diminishes any type of connection. So, if you keep engaging in it, there will be nothing left to salvage. The Gottman Institute found that contempt is one of the greatest predictors of divorce (Lisitsa, 2023). Promoting a culture of kindness and appreciation is the antidote to contempt.

☞ Playing the victim.
Talking about your hardship and emotions is a good thing, but if you position yourself as a hopeless victim, it implies that you have no

responsibilities. You remove control from yourself and place it on the other person, which creates an imbalance. Even if you were wronged, you need to communicate it, protect yourself with boundaries, and request change from others. All of this requires you to have a measure of control over what you do. So, recognize when you are playing the victim and perform a STOPP exercise.

☞ Playing the martyr.
People also often play the martyr card by saying how much they willingly sacrifice without receiving anything in return. Doing more for the other person and hoping that they will do the same is not enough. So, this tactic will get you nowhere. If you want things to change you need to make it clear. We need to remember that even in the closest relationships we need to ask for things and make sure that our significant other knows how we want to be treated. When you catch yourself in your martyr mode, perform a STOPP exercise or take a Time-Out.

☞ Begging/ people pleasing.
People who feel uncomfortable in conflict will very often want to avoid it by submitting or saying sorry, even though they don't mean it. If this is your way of dealing with conflict, you are on a fast track to depleting yourself emotionally. At some point something will "snap" and you might not be able to give in anymore, which can affect your ability to connect to others. I would suggest therapeutic sessions to work with your people pleasing Part and figure out its origin and what it needs in order to be dormant and calm. IFS therapy is very effective with these types of problems. So, acknowledge when you are people pleasing and perform a STOPP exercise or take a Time-Out.

☞ Passive aggression
Passive aggression comes in many shapes and sizes. We already discussed one example of it which was the silent treatment, but it can also appear as deliberate procrastination when it comes to things that are important

for your counterpart. Some people might politely start talking about subjects that trigger the other person.

Passive aggression is also giving backhand compliments, which means insulting someone with a phrase that could also be understood as a compliment. It can also be another form of indirect retaliation. It's a very toxic way of communicating with others. Before you can properly communicate, you need to formulate your arguments in your mind.

Think about what types of feelings and issues your passive aggression covers up. Talk about your emotions so that you can process them more easily and let other people see you in a more empathetic light. Perhaps you've been upset because the other person doesn't help you enough around the house. They might not know about it, so you will never get what you truly want, which is help around the house unless you discuss the problem directly. You need to be the one raising this concern so you can both think about how to resolve it. If you have tried to resolve the issue but the other person makes promises, that go unfulfilled, you need to present this person with consequences such as withdrawing your support around the house or asking them to move out. Please remember that consequences need to be communicated politely and firmly before you go through with them. If you don't communicate future consequences, it can also become passive aggressive communication.

☞ Instantly trying to fix the situation.

Searching calmly for a solution is a good thing to do, but some people want to fix things immediately and at any cost. If your partner asks for a Time-Out don't chase after them just to fix things. We need to accept that sometimes we'll go to bed angry and without a solution to a problem. This doesn't mean that we can't find a resolution the next day or the one after that. Recognize the anxious feeling that accompanies you when you want to fix things. This is your cue to perform a STOPP exercise or take a Time-Out.

☞ Criticism
Some people seem to think that if they criticize things or others enough, something will magically change. This is not the case, you might be left with no solution and further estrangement from your significant others. Instead, make sure to talk about your emotions. Make requests and come up with consequences for unfulfilled promises. Remember to catch yourself when you start to criticize and perform a STOPP exercise or take a Time-Out.

☞ Frequent & repeated discussion of the issues
Try to keep conversations brief when it comes to talking about the issue and move on to what could be the solution. If you catch yourself having a rant about the problem for prolonged periods of time, make sure to catch yourself after around 6-8 sentences. This much is enough to bring up the emotions and the problem itself.

☞ The need to be right.
Everyone has a different perspective on issues and situations. Arguing over who is right will not bring you any closer to the resolution. Instead, focus on validating each other's emotions and experience and finding future changes so that this problem doesn't resurface. In relationships there is no logic because emotions are not always logical. That is why the right and wrong type of thinking is not useful. Everyone has a different reality and unique perspective on the world. To have a good communication in relationships we need to allow for understanding of other's reality. When you realize you want to be "right" again, perform a STOPP exercise or take a Time-Out.

REFLECTION
These dysfunctional communication mechanisms can come in sets. Perhaps you yell first, and then you withdraw. Recognize your style and think about its origins. Did someone in your childhood home interact like this? Or maybe your mechanism came as a response to some

dysfunctional behavior performed at home? Now that you see what is not serving you well, you have the responsibility to change your ways for the sake of the people in your life, if not for yourself. You set a bad example for future generations and make your own life much more difficult if you continue on this path.

Self-regulation practices and mindfulness will be your friends on the journey to better communication skills. Start recognizing your problematic mechanisms and emotions. Think about the way it feels when you get angry, scared, or disrespected. Catch your emotions and Parts before they lead you to scream, withdraw, or blame.

* * *

It's not easy to take hard look at your behaviors and emotions, but you could enrich your life so much if you change your dysfunctional ways. My journey was mostly about angry Part and covered fear of not being respected and helpless. As a child I was tiny, and I had to speak out in anger to be respected and seen. I learned swearing quite early because I saw that it's scaring my bullies. I learned that with show of anger you can quickly gain respect or make other people fear you and that was much more appealing than feeling helpless. I had to recognize that getting angry as an adult no longer worked and that if I learn to communicate my feelings, set boundaries and ask for respect my angry Part stays dormant and happy. I of course needed a lot of breathing exercises and support from my partner, friends, and family. It's ok to say to your counterparty "please, bear with me for a second" if you are feeling Parts' invasion.

SUMMARY

In this chapter I've explained why communication is so important for us, especially when it comes to dating. We discussed emotional regulation, which is a vital part of good communication skills. Also, how to watch out for your biases and how to allow others to have their opinions and perspectives. Fundamental communication skills are connected to calmness and openness to others, which is why I included some common self-regulation strategies such as STOPP exercise and Time-Outs. We have also discussed dysfunctional and toxic communication strategies and patterns to help you identify if you might have some of them. For each example, I presented you with practical remedies.

Chapter 8:
Social Skills Curriculum

This chapter will define social skills, how they develop what can go wrong in social interactions, and how to improve. I'll also talk about my own experiences with gaining social skills through practice and provide an exercise that you should use to improve your social skills. Lastly, I'll give some tips surrounding conversation topics, social introductions, creation of your catch phrases, and choosing your audience.

Social skills are a set of verbal and non-verbal abilities that let you converse and connect to others for social, romantic, and networking purposes. If you have them, it means that you're able to convey what you want to say to another person efficiently. Nevertheless, you also need to consider what you want people to feel about you and about the content of your words. Social abilities are composed of tone of voice, facial expressions, gestures, and word choice. With these factors you can make people feel comfortable, angry, in love, confused and so many other emotions. Of course, words and actions can be taken out of context so we can't be directly responsible for other people's reactions and feelings. But you can provoke them and have some impact on them via our social skills.

To date joyfully and effectively, you need to polish your social skills so that you can show your true and best self to others. If you're struggling with dating because of shyness and lack of social skills and only try to wait until you can jump into a long-term relationship, it won't be long before the dating burnout will come knocking on your door. This isn't a healthy option for dating.

Socializing and public speaking are skills and not personality traits. This is a crucial thing to understand so that you can gladly embark on the journey of learning social skills. Social skills need to be practiced. Of course, some people are naturally better than others at socializing, but if you study and practice hard enough, you can match people at any level. Go out and mingle, see what works and what doesn't work in your social interactions, play with the strategies and, one day, you will find yourself on the way to having a committed relationship.

If you're suffering from social anxiety, perhaps it's time to reach out for professional help. But if you prefer to learn and transform by yourself, that's great as well! Tailored steps and regular Mindful Check-Ins are key to treatment of social phobia. Set up weekly goals, so that you can keep track of your progress and make socializing habitual. But be careful not to overdo it, if your brain gets too many stressful stimuli that aren't properly processed you might feel the need to step away from socializing altogether. You should make your steps safe enough and challenging enough so that you can see progress.

On a personal note, what really changed the game for me was moving to the other side of the world, travelling extensively, and working as a tour guide for five months in Amsterdam where I had to speak in front of 15 people three times a day. Me, who trembled and forgot her words during university presentations, happily chatted and presented in front of people. All it took was enough days of extensive practice and putting myself out there to see that my life wouldn't end if I talked. I wasn't experienced in public speaking and had lived in Amsterdam for less than a week, but you truly can fake it until you make it when it comes to social interactions. I was secretly terrified for the first week, but nobody knew!

And believe me, most of the time people are wrapped up in their own problems and appearances rather than super focused on judging your every move. Even if there are a few individuals that pick on you, or don't listen to you, they're not your audience and maybe you need to look for a more worthy one. There are many things that could go wrong in social interactions, especially with the current strong emphasis on political correctness. People can misunderstand you, react in multiple ways, judge you, or ignore you. We must be prepared for difficult situations in order to excel at communication and social skills.

The key is to be mindful of others and their emotions while not getting so preoccupied with the way you're presenting yourself that you go into a stress reaction. Remember that you can't please everyone, and you shouldn't aim to do so. If you feel reasonably comfortable and you're not insulting others, that's all you need for the foundation of your social skills and the rest of the tricks will come with time. The exercise below will allow you to practice your social skills in small steps.

* * *

EXERCISE: Social Butterfly
Start frequenting social events and visiting new places where people socialize or frequent such as:
- Meet up groups.
- Networking events.
- The mall.
- The park.
- Toast Master Class (public speaking and improv groups).
- Other classes or group activities (yoga, pottery, drawing, cycling, etc.).
- Book clubs.

Or try to set up a "friend date" through portals like Bumble BFF. Bumble Date has a subcategory called Bumble BFF to meet friends only. Set up a goal to visit those places 2-3 times a week. You can start with just a quick appearance and introducing yourself to at least 3 people at the gathering or having a quick one-hour coffee "friends date". Try to build up your skills and gradually increase your confidence. Don't expect this to become easy very quickly. Even I, who built up my own skills over the years to be able to speak in public with confidence and enjoyment, still have moments of insecurity and being left out. To mitigate that, I quickly reassure my inner Kid and move on to another person if I don't feel the connection building in the conversation.

Each week set yourself a new small achievable goal such as:
- Talk to one extra person.
- Stay at the event for another hour.
- Chat to a person you find attractive.
- Set up a "friend date" or a date with someone from the group (or at least offer it).
- Exchange social media or phone numbers with someone.

Be creative about your goals! Small goals will give you more confidence and more reasons to celebrate and keep going. This type of exercise can also bring you new connections that could turn into meaningful and fulfilling friendships, partnerships and/or relationships.

* * *

The social tips in the next section of this book will provide you with some practical tips and insights that I came up with based on my life experiences. Try them and see if they work for you. The section will discuss catchy topics of conversation, ways to enter a conversation, good social introductions, how to create your own catch phrase or a question and how to choose your audience.

Social Tips

1. Think about catchy topics that most people like and educate yourself about those genres, for example, psychology, recent events, hobbies, sports, books. What you choose will depend on what you enjoy and your usual audience. For me psychology and sex therapy are a default mode when I can't or don't want to think of anything else. Everyone is curious about it!

2. Make sure that you practice different ways of entering and developing conversations. Here are some examples for you to try:

- Single out one person and strike up a conversation instead of approaching a whole group at once.
- Start with introducing yourself to the most "accessible" and least "threatening" individuals. By threatening, I mean intimidating with their good looks and/or their expressive personality.
- If you find a conversation boring or intimidating, you can try to discretely bring up another subject or, if you have no interest in the person, you can also excuse yourself by going to the bathroom or expressing a need to grab another drink or to greet someone else.
- Try mirroring some of the body language of your counterpart. It shows people that you're actively listening to them. It can make others believe that you're creating a connection and that you empathize with them.
- Build up on your counterpart's opinions and stories instead of jumping from topic to topic. Summarize what was said and ask some questions.
- When your new acquaintance mentions some memories or facts about themselves, try to find something that relates to you and talk about your own experiences with a similar theme, situation, or emotion.
- Ask people about themselves. We love to see that other people care about what we think. Often, you can get away with just asking questions instead of thinking of specific topics or cleaver things to say.

3. Try different ways of introducing yourself; make sure that people can't miss your greeting and that it's a meaningful one. Don't abruptly get in front of people and violently steal the spotlight but choose your moment. Make sure that the person can hear you and see you properly. Some individuals will just murmur their name in the background so they will obviously be less noticeable and memorable. People remember first impressions and crucial information about you.

 e.g., "I'm Saskia the sex therapist of the group."
 or "I'm Tim, I'm friends with the organizer."

If you give additional information at the beginning, you make yourself look more accessible because people can already think of topics that they can raise with you. In the above examples, they already know that you're a sex therapist or a friend of the organizer.

4. If for example you're grumpy and having a bad day and you regret some actions or words, you can own up to it later on. People respect when we're upfront about our shortcomings. It can make us relatable and shows honesty. You can always start again with, "It was not my best day last week when I saw you!".

5. Think of phrases and ideas that catch attention. For example, my Australian ex and I were discovering the cultural differences between us and one of the main ones was European versus Australian architecture. It was hard for me here in Sydney without double-glazed windows and central heating, whereas for him it's just the way the world is. All my European readers can probably relate to this, that's why it's such an emotional topic in my friend circles.

One of ex-partner's go-to strategy while meeting my largely European social circles was to start up a discussion about this surprisingly controversial topic. You can see people become invested in this conversation very quickly because it's non-invasive enough, but the opinions on it can be strong and everyone can find out something new from the exchange. The catch phrase was: "So what do you guys think about Australian houses?" We didn't have to think of new topics for another half hour.

Think of some ideas that can be a balance of common knowledge and excitement. Something that is light and not too emotionally demanding. Even though the emotional response is strong when it comes to European versus Australian architecture, the topic is only houses and insulation. When you come up with an idea, figure out how you can raise this topic in a fun way, so your catch phrases can gain some shape.

Now is the time to test it! Don't get discouraged if it doesn't work, perhaps you're playing to the wrong audience. Obviously, the above catch phrase would not be as influential if he was talking to a group of South Americans or Southeast Asians. That brings us to the next point.

6. Audience:
If you want to successfully blend in anywhere, you need to consider your audience. What's their main occupation? What are their culture and life experiences? People sometimes don't like the question "Where are you from?" because it seems to be creating barriers.

But I think it creates more topics of conversation and connects you through the exchange of experiences. It really depends on how you choose to lead the conversation after that question.

There's a big war on stereotypes these days. We clearly are trying to fight the bias in our minds which is good, but sometimes it can go too far. It goes into extremes when we politicize speech and don't allow mistakes or opinions other than our own. Obviously, not everyone is stereotypical, but the truth is that being raised in a certain country, or a community has a massive impact on us. The more I travel, the more the stereotypes prove to be somewhat true, and I realize that each society has a different set of easily recognizable traits.

For example, in my opinion, Polish people drink a lot of vodka, and they're very honest. There are obviously individuals that don't drink it at all, and there are some shy and not upfront Poles, but the majority of my interactions can confirm that brutal honesty and vodka consumption is very frequent. Our brain works in stereotypes and this ability helped us during hunter gatherer times to distinguish foe and the enemy. It's no longer as applicable, but it's what helped us survive and make sense of things quickly. After we use the subconscious stereotypes, we can choose to override them mindfully or use them to describe something or someone.

That's why the most common questions are "What do you do for living?" and "Where are you from?" We want to make sense of who our audience is and how we can engage them so that we can check for similarities and emotional connection.

SUMMARY

This chapter explains what social skills are, how to improve them and how to approach the learning process. I also speak about my beginnings to encourage you to stick with developing your social skills. I hope you'll take your social and conversational abilities seriously and practice with the exercise included in the chapter.

Lastly, I presented you with some practical tips that helped me greatly on my social journey. You can read more about dating social skills in the second part of the book. Here I would like you to get comfortable with basic friendly social interactions that are the foundation of creating any type of meaningful relationships.

Also, if you have a good social support system like friends and family, there's a better potential for higher self-esteem, confidence and building new interpersonal and intrapersonal skills. Cherishing social interactions outside of the relationship can also mitigate codependency and creates balance that is needed to safely invite a partner into your life. The longest study performed to check for factors contributing to quality of life and happiness found that a significant denominator is the quality of our relationships with other people (Waldinger & Schulz, 2023).

Chapter 9:
Dodge the Dating Burnout

In this chapter we discuss a phenomenon called dating burnout or dating fatigue. Next, I'll help you diagnose if you have dating fatigue via an exercise. I give you 11 top tips to look after yourself while dating and to avoid dating burnout. We will also talk about the mindset needed to keep healthy while dating and how to enjoy solitude and avoid loneliness.

Dating burnout is a state where you dread your next date. You perceive your dating life as a necessary evil so that you can get into a long-term relationship and get it over with. When you experience dating fatigue, lack of fulfillment and a sense of pointlessness also creeps in. It can make you feel anxious, tired, bored, angry, annoyed, and depressed. Everyone gets similar symptoms at times, but you then need to recognize if it could be coming from a different place like work stress or family drama. Another practice that can increase the probability of dating burnout is hyper fixating on dating, when you treat your dates like a meeting to tick boxes and move on to the next one, or if you're so absorbed in having more dates that you neglect other parts of your life like your social engagements, work, or self-care. This can deplete you quickly, so it's important to monitor yourself and avoid such spirals.

If your negative thoughts are mainly related to your love life, you might be experiencing dating burnout. To skillfully dodge dating burnout, you need to know if you have it or if you are on the way to this state of mind. To acknowledge if that problematic state took over, active daters should occasionally perform the following exercise.

* * *

EXERCISE: Dating Burnout Diagnostics
Answer these questions:
- Is dating interfering with your life and schedule in any major way?
- Do you tend to drop other commitments like social gatherings or self-development projects to attend dates?
- Do you feel triggered, tired, or annoyed every time you think about going on a date?
- Do you sometimes think that dating is pointless, so why do you even bother?

If you answered "yes" to any of these questions, your dating style might be unhealthy. I encourage you to take a step back and focus on introspective, self-care and self-improvement before you reengage in dating.

* * *

11 Tips to Dodge Dating Burnout

1. Be Aware of Dating Burnout
Even though dating is a numbers game, we can quickly burnout if we overcommit ourselves to a mindless date count per week. When it stops being enjoyable, it becomes a chore and here comes burnout! If you know that such a phenomenon exists, you can keep a look out for it. If you're more irritable, less fulfilled and run down because of your dating life, you can self-diagnose with a dating burnout. People who experience it often think of dating as hard, pointless and in general something that must be done rather than a fun and exciting activity.

2. Treat It Like any Other Area of Your Life
If you're overwhelmed with social commitments, take a step back and have some "me time." If work gets on your nerves, perhaps it's time for a vacation. And if you have been on so many dates to find "the one" that

you can't remember the names of people that you have met, it could be a sign that you need to refocus and take a breather. Set up your dates in a way that is comfortable for you without impacting the rest of your life. Focus on one person at a time to regain the balance in your dating pattern. If you're on a dating spree and mindlessly spending time with countless random individuals, you're not being mindful.

3. Use Mindfulness

We already know how important mindfulness is when it comes to most areas of our lives. It's especially so in dating. If you can give your date undivided attention for a short period of time, you can really give this relationship a "go" and be 100 percent sure if you want to pursue something more or to end the contact. If you're attentive just half of the time you might be wasting your and their time.

4. Remember to Pay Attention to Your Body and Mind.

They will give you signs such as anxiety, anger, sadness, negative thinking, lack of purpose and fulfilment or positive butterflies in your stomach. If you recognize those, it will be much easier for you to recognize dating fatigue.

5. Treat Dating as a Fun Activity.

Approach dating as something that you can enjoy or at least something that will teach you some useful life skills. I didn't necessarily get excited about the whole education process and the fact that I had to wake up for one of my courses at 3 a.m. but I was excited about the knowledge and opportunities that this process gave me. You can look at dating in a similar way. If it's just empty means to an end, no wonder you're feeling depleted and hating the whole dating world. Remember that no one is making you date. If you choose to do it, make the most of it and show up with the right attitude, even if it's stressful.

6. Drop the Victim Mentality.

After countless rejections, we can sometimes lose track of who we are and here comes another emotional flooding. Victim mode is one of your protective Parts; it wants to blame someone else for the way you feel. So, you might develop biases that hold you back. For example, have you ever told yourself: I'm never the girlfriend or I'm always the friendzone guy? It's your internal victim at its best. When you get into that zone you forget that you probably, at some point, rejected others as well. To go against this unconscious bias, make sure to take the control kindly but firmly away from your internal Victim. Explain to it that you're in charge of your choices, and that you can soothe yourself without blaming others or playing victim.

7. Protect Yourself with Boundaries.

Show people how to treat you by letting them know about your needs, which means creating external boundaries. Make sure your dates know what you're looking for. If it's a long-term relationship don't settle for half measures and people that just want something casual. Remember not to judge people by their relationship preferences, it's not their fault that they don't want the same things you do. By adopting objective and non-judgmental perspective, you create healthy internal boundaries and prevent victim mentality from popping up.

8. Don't Play "What If" Games.

Did you ever plan your future with someone that you've just met or haven't even met? Future telling or wondering what would happen if you met later in life or in different circumstances will also send you on the express way to a burnout. That's because you're putting plenty of your emotional energy into things that don't have-- and might never have-- any substance. If it was supposed to happen, it would be already happening for you. Period. And if it's supposed to happen in the future, you're not achieving anything by overthinking the situation and draining yourself of your energy via unhealthy ruminations.

9. Keep Balance Between Creating a Window of Opportunity and Knowing When to Call it Quits.

Dating also stops being enjoyable if you lack options and you're unwilling to put yourself out there because you're waiting for someone to magically appear. Today, it's perfectly fine for a woman to make a first step, so there are no excuses, ladies.

I've met a lot of beautiful, smart, and successful women who don't have a partner even though they long for one. The problem is all of them were waiting for a prince charming to come sweep them off their feet instead of actively seeking him out.

Make sure that you make some effort and create a window of opportunity, but if the other person doesn't extend their hand, it's time to move on. If you notice that often you're overstaying your welcome or too weak to leave an unhealthy situation, it's time for a change.

Be transparent about your needs and don't hold on to someone who won't ever meet them. Stop contacting someone who doesn't reciprocate this energy.

10. Invest in Relationships in a Smart Way.
By investing I mean showing your interest in someone. It's okay to show that you're interested in a person even early on, obviously not to express your love but curiosity doesn't have to mean love. If your date does not reciprocate this energy, you can easily take it away.

Making small gestures will let you know if this person is worth your time and effort. It's a basic principle of investment. You give a little and wait for it to come back to you in some way. If it doesn't, even after you make your needs clear, it's a definite cue that you need to dust yourself off and try elsewhere.

Giving attention to someone or displaying your interest is not only about giving but receiving. Giving provides you with an opportunity to test others and this knowledge helps you to make the best decisions. So, you might give a compliment or show affection but what you receive is intel, it's still an exchange. If you're too afraid to give, you have no cards to play and you're in a passive position in which you either don't care enough or you're at the mercy of others who might not have the best intentions. Be an active party and, when you know how to give and receive, it might even become an enjoyable search.

11. Don't Date from a Place of Lack
Desperation can be very noticeable so remember your worth and that you have options. Don't settle because you believe that you're not good enough to get anyone better. Work on your self-esteem, confidence, and other internal issues first.

* * *

The growing numbers of partner options and rejections that we have to endure can also prompt dating fatigue. We're presented with so many options, possibilities, and images that it can be hard to choose. There are many studies on how the increase in options can make us less likely to make a decision (Pronk & Denissen, 2019; Scheibehenne et al., 2010). The increasing number of rejections that we need to perform creates the perspective of lack and failure in our mind and that, in turn, can get us emotionally depleted, numb, more likely to reject again and more likely to associate dating with negativity.

To avoid such a reaction, we need to be mindful and centred each step of the way and to move at a pace that allows us better balance and control. If you don't focus on your date and on your behaviors, thoughts, and feelings, and you're not really giving it a true go, you slip into your automatic patterns of behavior. That means you're more likely to reject someone who could be a potential partner or a friend, and you lack the capacity to try and develop connection.

At a certain stage when you have dated so much with no results, or you swiped left so many times you might have already gotten into this "rejection bias". Other studies, however, have shown that more options can also increase choice in some cases (Scheibehenne et al., 2010). So, findings are inconclusive in this area.

Nevertheless, if you notice that looking for a date has become burdensome, take a step back and check your internal boundaries, life balance and general health and go back to the dating scene when you feel emotionally better.

Dating and the whole process of finding someone suitable is not everyone's cup of tea. Perhaps you want to skip all this hard work and get to the "good bits"? I'm sorry to disappoint you, but you can't. And it's not an Adult thing to do to keep telling yourself: "If I could just only skip this one!" Sounds like a Kid who doesn't like Math's. Tell your internal Kid that a Grown Up is taking the steering wheel. I hope I have skillfully helped you to get over yourself and try a more mindful approach.

If you consistently return to the skills that you developed, especially with the first part of the book, you should be an expert in dodging dating burnout. Just like with career or social burnouts, it's all about self-care, self-reflection, and boundaries. If you have all of those in place, you can safely and confidently date and find the right person or people for you!

We know that good and healthy relationships can make us better people who are more satisfied with life. So that should be your motivation to reject all the options that make you feel like less than. There's no point in staying in a bad relationship to avoid being alone. Some singles feel loneliness and longing for a partner. It's absolutely normal to have those feelings. Nevertheless, I encourage you to embrace your single life as well, because the sadness that comes with feeling lonely will get you onto a fast track to dating fatigue. If you enter a relationship from a place of hating your life, it will be very noticeable to the other person. Of course, some unhappy singles will find their match and will lead a happier life with them. Isn't it just nicer to cherish your whole life rather than just parts of it? Being by yourself doesn't have to be bad and sad.

Being happily alone is called solitude. When you're in this state, you feel connected and well, even though there's no one around you. It's a much different experience from feeling alone. You can feel lonely in a room full of people and even with a partner or a friend at times, when we feel unheard, misunderstood, and treated poorly. Practice solitude so that you can access your inner Adult state and internal self-esteem. This in turn will mitigate the risks of Dating Fatigue. Perform the exercise below to practice solitude.

* * *

EXERCISE: Solitude AKA Connected by Yourself
Practice this exercise not only at your lows, but also when you're feeling good while alone. The more you perform it, the more it becomes anchored inside of you, making it easier to access this state of mind.

I find it works well when you have a nice view. Maybe you want to have a seat next to a window or go to a park nearby. Go inside of your thoughts and feelings and acknowledge what and who is coming to visit you when it omes to your Parts. Now, think about things that truly matter in your life like family, friends, your new project, your work, your pet or even your apartment. You can also acknowledge the beauty of the world that surrounds you. Feel the connection to nature and other people. Focus on those themes and see how they make you feel. Where is the connected sensation in your body? This is your feeling of solitude, so remember it for next time.

Think about how important those things are and that, although they may be absent right now, you can still feel the connection going through your body. You might be thinking that it's a gratitude exercise, but it's more than that. I want you to put that gratitude aside for a moment and focus on the sensation of togetherness and bonding. Feelings can be practiced, even though they come and go. Sometimes we can evoke them. I often compare emotions to past ghosts who possess us at times but can also be summoned if you create a good relationship with them.

Similarly, if you feel solitude, you can also summon happiness by acknowledging when you're truly happy or realizing that there are awesome things around you that can cause happiness. That's why gratitude journals are so influential. Being optimistic, positive, happy, and connected is a habit, not something that some people automatically possess.

* * *

I personally have had a big journey when it comes to loneliness and solitude. I left my country early on in life and it was not entirely prompted by my wants and excitement. I just finished highschool and didn't get into artschool so my options were to stay in Poland and start a low paying job and studies that I didn't want or go to Australia to start a new life and rethink my direction. Leaving meant also that I had to break up with my partner at the time and that I had to flip my whole life up side down. My parents had financial issues at the time so they really wanted me to go and have a better life in Sydney. At first loneliness was overwhelming, but I got use to it and I started enjoying, then unimaginable freedom of being so independent. This led me to more travels and enjoyment of solitude.

Eventhough I was enjoying the independence I was constantly missing romance. Longing for a partner is present in most people's life. Client's often ask how to get over feeling lonely and start enjoying the single life. I usually say to that: "you can't delete your feelings". If you will not accept loneliness and choose to enjoy your life in spite of it you will despise single life.

Before getting into my current mindset I was making a lot of the mistakes that I have mentioned above. I was blaming the world and that stopped me from improving myself. I wasn't meeting anyone interesting for long periods of time and I was settling for good enough options because I didn't believe I can find someone I truly want. The moment I focused on personal growth, good communication and regular training people that I wanted just appeared in front of me in a short period of time. I'm not saying there was magic involved, but the person that you truly want will resonate with the best version of you. When you become it or constantly strive to be better it's much easier to attract that person. Burnout will also not invade a person that is so self-actualized.

SUMMARY

We have defined dating burnout and how to recognize it. I have also given you 11 tips for preventing and treating dating burnout. In addition, we discussed the importance of accepting the loneliness that can come with singlehood and how to exchange it with solitude. With the given exercises you should be able to switch to experiencing solitude instead of feeling alone. I hope these tips and exercises have given you a window into yourself and your dating style in order to monitor and treat dating fatigue.

Chapter 10:
Types of Relationships for Your Consideration

I'll focus on Western societies and contemporary culture surrounding the process of finding a suitable partner. I'll bring up different types of romantic connections that we can create instead of having a committed relationship. Third, we'll discuss different types of relationships, such as monogamous and polyamorous. In addition, I'll examine the different ways people choose to have these relationships, depending on their emotions and needs. Lastly, I'll provide you with some terms and definitions that will make things clearer for you and will help you decide which type of connection interests you.

CASUAL DATING

The dating world is ever changing depending on technological and medicinal discoveries such as contraception. This prompted more sexual equality and gave women the ability to choose when and if to get pregnant. It used to be about stability and security, but now there's more wiggle room for pleasure, experimentation and choosing a different pathway rather than a typical hetero/monogamous relationship. Currently you can pick from so many different options. The line between taken and single has blurred so we invented different terms to navigate dating life.

Relations where one or both people don't want to commit and create a relationship, we call "casual". Often if you been through difficult times, break ups or are simply not in a headspace for creating anything serious, that's the option for you. Relationships are very emotionally demanding and time consuming which is why many people would opt for this type of relation instead. There is nothing wrong with wanting to just enjoy the company of the other person without committing in terms of support and consistent meetings.

The problems with this type of dating begin if we are not sincere about our intentions and lead people on. If you choose to engage in casual relationships, remember to be transparent and create some boundaries around this loose arrangement to avoid uncomfortable situations. If you label things as "casual" that's what they will be, and you most likely won't get consistent attention and support. Nevertheless, even if you are casually seeing someone, you should be able to ask for some things within reason. Simple signs of respect and being treated as a friend are the bare minimum that every person who is dating you casually should display.

My advice for you casual daters is – monitor your emotions and acknowledge when a certain relation is playing on your mind. If you feel undervalued, used, sad or angry, it could be the time to voice your concerns or to leave this arrangement. I know plenty of people who stayed in some relations because they were hoping for more and that's a quick way to hurt yourself. To happily date casually, you need self-awareness and knowing when to stand up for yourself. If you are capable of doing it, then you are ready to have fun with your casual dates!

Types of Casual Relationships:

☞ Situationship:
This is a type of a relation where you keep in touch with your romantic mate, and you might even be acting like you're in a relationship but one or both of you don't want to be exclusive or to "put a label on it". There's an emotional connection present between the people who engage in a Situationship.

☞ Dating:
It's an early stage of a potential relationship where it's generally acceptable to not be exclusive because the two people are still figuring out if they would like to progress into something more serious. It can be, however, sometimes looked down upon to be dating multiple people at the same time. Depending on who you ask, you can hear glorification or condemnation of dating multiple individuals. I've heard people say this is appropriate for men but not women. So there is clearly a double standard. But if others aren't hurting me or other people with their actions. Who am I to judge?

☞ Friends with Benefits:
In this situation the focus is on sexual gratification and both parties agree not to label their connection as a relationship. They might still be friends in the outside world and engage with the same social circles, but they don't display their affection publicly. It seems very similar to a Situationship but the players are less emotionally connected.

☞ A Booty Call:
This is a person that you might call for sexual gratification only.

☞ One-Night Stand:
This is a casual one-time sexual encounter.

The top of the list is filled with types of relationships that involve some commitment and emotional connection or at least potential for deepening the relationship. The bottom of the list is taken by very meaningless encounters between people, which can often be dehumanizing and unfulfilling when it comes to emotional needs, even though they can be adventurous and satisfying for people when it comes to sexual experience. Nevertheless, plenty of people still hope for just one good, connected, and stable relationship.

MONOGAMY

Monogamy is a prevalent way for people to experience relationships, but the concept has been subjected to evolution. Monogamy used to equal marriage, but currently many people choose not to marry and are happy in their partnerships without "making it official" with the government and/or God.

The biggest challenge in monogamy seems to be staying faithful and connected. When the honeymoon phase passes and hormones wear off, relationships can stagnate, and couples can lose the pull towards one another. Nevertheless, people can also become so comfortable that leaving starts to be too difficult, and the motivation is insufficient to make a change. Then they find themselves in therapy offices like mine. We forget that a long-term relationship is not the same as the short-term blast in the beginning, so we need to rely on other things.

The honeymoon phase is easy because hormones drive our behavior by getting us excited, but later, when there's fewer of them, because we're more comfortable and secure, we tend to forget to put in the effort that used to be driven by the hormonal changes in our brains. To be a remarkable and connected couple you need consistency in creating your connection, plenty of communication and honesty. Sexual attraction and connection are like flowers in a garden that need to be watered and cared for.

POLYAMORY AND OPEN RELATIONSHIPS

People who have multiple partners are a minority but it's a pathway which is explored by more and more people, especially in younger generations. This type of dating is largely misunderstood and labeled deviant and unnatural. I found that people who prefer to go into these types of arrangements have a different mentality when it comes to creating connections. In polyamorous folk I observed the ability to give romantic attention to a few people at the same time and a greater need for variety. I also realized that cross-dating between monogamous and polyamorous people seems to be difficult as the two worlds differ in their complexities.

In monogamy the main issues are keeping up the spark and successful sexual connection and excitement in the relationship. Whereas in an open partnership the problems can arise from jealousy and imbalance between partners when it comes to dividing time, attention, or other resources (Kauppi,

2021). Especially when there's a new relationship or an infatuation on the horizon, this phenomenon is called New Relationship Energy (NRE). NRE is a feeling that we get when we start to date someone new, the excitement, infatuation, and a lot of butterflies in our bellies. A long-term stable relationship is not as filled with hormonal changes in the brain as is the fresh feeling of new love. During this transitory stage many poly relationships can go through turmoil and imbalance. That's why it's so important that the person who is dating someone new is mindful of the needs of their long-term partner. This type of dating and relationships can give you the opportunity to experience the NRE repeatedly, but it also can get very complex. There are many different ways to be in an open relationship. To give you more insight on polyamory and other open options, I include some definitions.

☞ Monogamish:
Colloquially used to refer to relationships that are romantically monogamous but also allow for agreed-upon pursuits of other people. Sometimes it will only be, for example, a permission to flirt.

☞ Swinging:
If you're a couple and want to slightly open your relationship for fun, then swinging could be an option for you. Swingers often perceive sex or other forms of fun such as voyeurism (watching other people have sex) as recreation. Swingers do not usually engage in additional relationships but will instead have casual encounters with other couples in swinger clubs. They might also be friends with those couples. The clubs welcome couples and single women who often join the couples, however, this culture is still not incredibly open to single men. Swinging began with 'wife-swapping' and excluded sexual contact between two men. It's still not common to include contact between men.

☞ Open Relationship:
Describing a relationship as 'Open' is a very broad description. It means that some romantic or sexual contact with others is allowed within

agreed-upon boundaries. It's mostly open to casual sex and most couples would not start new committed relationships. Dating and kissing may be acceptable, but sex may not be or having sex with others is allowed, but only when traveling or at some events. The possibilities and combinations used to create open relationships are endless.

☞ Polyamory

Polyamory describes having simultaneous meaningful and emotionally committed relationships with people who may or may not also be partners. It also depends on how you want to play it out. You need to establish if your partners want to meet each other. Also, if you want a hierarchical structure where you have a primary (most important and committed) relationship and other secondary, or tertiary. Or if you want a non-hierarchical structure where you give room for growth to every relationship which you have and commit equally. Dividing time and attention between partners in an appropriate way is very important in this type of love life arrangement.

☞ Mono-Poly

Another arrangement is where one person is polyamorous and the other prefers to stay monogamous. There's plenty of criticism towards this type from the monogamous community and from polyamorous people. Some will see this kind of relationship as abusive and a monogamous person as a victim. However, this arrangement also works for a lot of people.

☞ Polyfidelity

A derivative of Polyamory, where there is exclusivity within a certain group of people, and it entails a promise to not create any additional relationships. So, for example if you have two partners, you promise them that you will not be seeing anyone else. You're faithful to two people.

☞ Metamours

People who are connected through being in a relationship with the same person but are not sexually and emotionally involved. For example, if woman has two boyfriends and those boyfriends are not in a relationship with each other, they are metamours. They might know each other but some people are more comfortable with not knowing their metamours.

☞ Polycule
Group of people connected through a variety of romantic relationships in which they are involved by being a partner or a metamour.

☞ Triad
Three people who are in a relationship together. Also known as a throuple.

☞ Quad
Four people who are in a relationship together.

☞ Pod
A polycule that consists of more than four people.

If the arrangement that you're in starts to play around in your head in a negative way and you make yourself stay just because you feel strongly for this person, it's good to reconsider your options. You can strengthen your boundaries with that person and make sure that you're protected. Presenting other people with reasonable consequences for their behavior should not be thought of as a threat. Presenting consequences is like presenting different choices.

If your date wants a casual relationship with no labels, but you are a labels person, there's no point in pretending that you want to date casually too. In that case you can clearly state, without judging the other person, that you'll need to leave the situation if there's no label. Your date can decide if they want to part ways with you or if they would like to go into a relationship. We can't make ourselves want something to fulfill others' expectations. There's nothing less arousing and appealing for us than being forced into something that we dislike, by others or by our Kid Parts wanting to people please. On the other hand, if you're forcing yourself into a serious relationship prematurely, you might hurt your partner and yourself as well.

Honesty can be your greatest asset while dating. If you're honest with yourself and others, instead of listening to your NRE hormonal changes or popular beliefs, then it's much safer for you to navigate those dating waters. Think: "What is truly healthy and good for me right now?" Be open to new experiences and exploring different dating and relationship arrangements but Check-In with your body and mind, ask them what you truly want and need at each stage.

Apart from dating I have some experience when it comes to situationships. It was never a healthy experience and I don't think it's functional for other people either because in this type of connection one or both people bend or break their boundaries and don't get their needs met. First time I've decided to enter a situationship it was with one of my ex partners. I would not call him my boyfriend anymore because internally I knew that we do not fit together and there is no future for this relation, nevertheless I wasn't dating anyone else, and I still had feelings for him. I was also too proud to call it a relationship because I lost trust in him after he was unable to support me in hardship. He was hoping that I'll come around and I was taking my revenge. Now I regret the resentment and the need to "get even", it didn't help anyone.

Second time around I was the one hoping for more. In this scenario, I didn't last very long. The guy I was dating at the time was only inviting me to stay over and would rather watch footy than speak to me. He was also hung up on his ex partner. I have requested a change a in behavior and said that I won't be coming over anymore and that if he wanted to see me he can invite me for an actual date. After that I haven't heard from him much, only sporadically he would resurface to perhaps again check the "ground" or perhaps get some attention. I don't blame him for that, surely some Part of him needed something from me.

Maybe you can see a trend where situationships are not healthy for anyone because they require one or both partners to bend or break their boundaries. Even if you feel like you are enjoying yourself perhaps there is some deeper work for you to do if you can't bring yourself closer to the person that you have feelings for. Or if you can't let go of a person even though you know they want more from you than you can give.

HOMOSEXUAL DATING & RELATIONSHIPS

In this book I focus on heterosexual dating because that's where my personal expertise lies, and I mostly coach heterosexual people on dating. Nevertheless, I believe that a lot of information in this book can be applied to homosexual dating. In my line of work, I also help plenty of LGBTQIA+ folk to resolve their love life and sexual problems. Homosexual relationships are also divided in similar ways to heterosexual ones, they can be monogamous, but polyamory is also common.

If you're a homosexual reader or unsure about your sexuality and want to experiment with dating the same sex, I would recommend reaching out to your local LGBTQIA+ community. You can do that through social media or seeking out local events. You can also use the apps for same sex dating and socializing purposes like Grindr. Nevertheless, plenty of other dating apps include an option to look for same sex dates.

It's also good to know that abuse in homosexual relationships has more implications than the one occurring in heterosexual relationships. Some homosexuals will be less likely to report abuse because of social stigma and not wanting to be "outed" to their friends and family by the abusive partner. Some people will also consider the abuse normal because they lack experience in homosexual relationships. Society can also be unsupportive to such victims whether they report or not. It's important to keep abusive signs in your mind while dating.

SUMMARY

This chapter explored different relationship arrangements and structures so that you can pick one that suits you. We discussed the difference between being in a relationship and having a loose casual relationship. In addition, we explored differences between monogamy, polyamory, and other open relationship options. Finally, we touched on the homosexual dating world.

As you can see there are a few different dating worlds with their own glossaries. Now that you know what the options are, you can consider what you would ultimately like to have in your life. I encourage people to go into certain arrangements with a wholehearted YES! instead of doubts. This doesn't mean that healthy exploration can't be included.

PART 1: DATER KNOW THYSELF – SUMMARY
To date in a healthy way, you need to find a balance between enjoying the process itself and being mindful. We date for many different reasons like wanting a relationship, physical connection, sexual connection, company or to pass time. Whatever your reasons, you can't do it for very long if you're unprepared for rejection. Resilience keeps you centered and fulfilled even during the uncertainty that dating brings. Also, if you preplanned everything, for example that it will take you six months to find a suitable partner and then another six to move in together and maybe a year after you will have children, you might be surprised. Expect the unexpected.

This part was designed to prepare you for the dating life. Experiences and relationships can teach us many valuable lessons, but we also need to do some groundwork through introspection. If you make the same mistakes when it comes to choosing a partner, handling yourself during discussions or arguments and creating a healthy nourishing relationship dynamic, perhaps you need some inner work. Try to gather the lessons from the past to create a better future through action and changing your dating and partnership patterns.

Life is unpredictable and we need to learn to adjust. Even though I've included the Perfect Partner List Exercise it doesn't mean that you should come to every date with one and leave straight after you find that one tick can't be checked off. Dating can also lead to friendships and networking, so use this opportunity to practice open-mindedness. Perhaps you should also reassess your list for rigidity and too high expectations. If you treat it like a chore, it will become one and your dates may sense this. Rather than treating dating like a necessary evil, consider it a fun activity that adds to your life!

Part II:
Dating from A to Happily-Ever-After

Chapter 11: Meet Your Date

In this chapter we explore various ways to meet your dates. We review the most direct approach, which is organic search. Then we explore third-party involvement options like speed dating, and blind dates set up by family or friends, matrimonial agencies, and new social movements and social experiments. Lastly, we talk about online dating. I'll provide you with some practical hints and information to navigate each option.

The dating pool can be truly enormous if you know where and how to look and that gives you many possibilities. This is both good and bad; if you want to make the most of your options, mindfulness is the key. If you override the burnout and rejection bias, you're free to explore and give each option and chance.

There are many people who would like to be in a relationship but dislike dating and don't even try to put themselves out there. Unfortunately, the right person won't just fall out of the sky. If you want to have a love life, you need to go out there and get it. That is why I suggest letting your friends and family know that you are actively searching. Perhaps your loved ones can help you out on this journey either with matchmaking or at least with some useful information about your current crush. It's ultimately a numbers game, so you need to meet a certain amount of people to be able to make your decision if you're not one of the lucky few that scored their compatible life partner on the first try. Here are some options for you to consider.

Direct and Third-Party Approaches:

☞ Organic Search

You can opt for meeting someone just out and about, for example through friends, at a store or mall, in a park, at a meet-up, at work or school. This type of search can require courage because people don't automatically know that you're romantically interested in them. One of you needs to make a move that can make things clearer.

Historically, in heterosexual relationships the man was supposed to be the one to make the first step, but the world has changed, and more women are comfortable approaching men. Also, to approach someone doesn't need to mean to be very forward. If you start up a simple conversation about the weather, it can quickly change into flirting and an exchange of numbers. Rejection by a person that we find attractive is strongly linked to our self-esteem and body image and those can get a scratch or two if we don't have boundaries in place.

If you're shy and afraid of rejection, you can always use some excuse to talk to your handsome stranger! The damsel-in-distress pickup doesn't get outdated. If you're holding too much, perhaps someone can help you out with your coat; maybe you dropped a book by "accident" or you're looking for a reception desk?

Asking for help can work for guys too, once you have the person's attention and they don't seem like they are in a rush, you're in! There's no harm in small favors, real or imagined. We work with reciprocity, that way we distinguish friend from foe. When we help someone, we invest in them and what we invest in we tend to care about more. Studies have shown that if we put more effort into something, we tend to see higher perceived value in it because we like to mistake effort for value (Kim & Labroo, 2011).

Also, if someone gives you a hand, all the more reason to offer them a coffee or a drink. Later, you can make a joke about how your falling book wasn't that accidental after all. It can be flattering to the other person that you went through that thought process to arrive at this type of a plan of action just to get their attention.

Even if you're thinking: I'm a strong and independent person. I don't need help! And maybe you don't, but it's not about needing, rather about wanting. If you want someone, asking for a small favor can be your route to meeting them, and you might give them the gift of feeling helpful and needed.

This initial stage can be simultaneously intimidating and exciting. No other option has this intriguing stage of figuring out if there's a romantic connection. All the following options entail that there is or could be some attraction present because you're already on a date and looking for romance. But in an organic search you start as perfect strangers and romantic attraction needs to be properly shown, so that your encounter can move on to an official date or at least another meeting. Practicing organic searching can also rapidly increase your social skills because it requires some boldness and going outside of your comfort zone.

Nevertheless, I can see a new trend in contemporary society, namely men are nowadays labeled as "creepy" for the direct approach. Believe me I had my fair share of creepy people calling me so I know how annoying it can be to decline all the offers. However, I try to give everyone a benefit of the doubt before I implement my boundaries. By jumping to conclusions in that way we also create another trend, men are not approaching women as much anymore because of fear of being called creepy.

Many attractive men that I have dated or just interacted with have mentioned this. They would wait for women to approach them or use other means to meet their prospective dates. I have also met many women complaining that men today don't approach them and therefore they don't feel as feminine. To promote healthy direct interactions, please use your boundaries to gently reject others and not display disgust or yell out "creep!" every time. Of course if you find yourself in danger, by all means, yell as much as you can. But also if you are approaching someone respect their personal space and display courtesy and respect towards them.

If you are approaching someone restrain from physical contact, you just met the person. Stick to simple conversation and don't ask very personal questions. Don't try to turn the interaction into a date, but rather have a chat, ask a few questions and get their contact details so you can text or call that person later. Small steps are more appealing, especially to mentally healthy and stable individuals. Make sure that you don't approach people in enclosed places or corner them somewhere, keep appropriate distance, make sure to smile and let them know with your gestures and posture that you have friendly intentions. The better you explain your intentions the more this person will feel at ease, that's why excuses such as asking for help are so effective. But if you skillfully and confidently express your interest in setting up a date, you can have the same effect.

☞ Speed Dating:

It's a lovely idea that can give you a quick overview of available singles in the area. If it's heterosexual speed dating, there is a group of men and a group of women. Everyone has a set amount of time to spend with each participant from the opposite group. After the event, you write down who you would like to see again and, if the interest is mutual, the organizers will provide both of you with each other's contact details.

This type of dating calls for quick-witted conversation. My advice is to come up with a clever and short introduction. If you can make your speed date laugh during those few minutes, you're ahead of the others. Instead of just stating your job and a hobby, dress it up as something worth discussing.

E.g., "I'm a construction worker, I save people every day from death by collapsing ceilings."

Or

"I'm a hairdresser, so mainly I treat people's psychological issues."

Professions are the most common subject, so expect work related questions. If you answer with a clever joke or offer a small insight into what it's really like for you every day, people can relate to you, and it sparks more conversation. When you smile together, even if the joke is dry, it's a sign that the initial ice is melting. In the beginning, both of you can be shy and nervous. You can also make room for a compliment!

Meeting many people on the same night can be draining because you need to remember enough information about them to make your final decision. Make sure to take a breather. It's fine if you want to tell your dates that you feel overwhelmed. I consider myself composed and good at conversations and even for me it was challenging.

☞ Blind Date

If you decide to let your family and friends in on your search, you can create a new pool of options. If your close circle is the meddling type, they might set you up. Some people are uncomfortable with this option. If you're okay with a blind date, make sure that you ask plenty of questions before you say "yes" to a meeting.

A photo of your blind date would be useful, even though it's called "blind date." Most of the time we date others who are similar in age, attractiveness, and educational background. If you aren't attracted to the person and you want to be friends, there's no point in calling it a romantic date and getting the other person's hopes up. You can arrange a friendly meeting instead. It can save you the complications that come from rejections. Perhaps you want to preserve the surprise element of "blind dates" and trust your loved one's gut? This is also an option.

☞ Matrimonial Agencies and Advertisements

These are places to advertise your partner search or let a matchmaker find someone that could be suitable for you. Those are not as widely used as they used to be. Now, matchmaking is taken over by online dating, but there are still plenty of agencies that will offer comprehensive personality tests to pair you up.

☞ New Movements and a Social Experiment

People are starting to get more creative about meeting a potential mate. In an era where it's hard to find a committed partner, people have been thinking of platforms and events for other like-minded individuals who want something serious. Communities have been created on social media platforms to say "Hi" to others and tell them what you're looking for.

One of those communities was created via a social experiment. It was the first-time organizers connected people in Australia, USA, Canada, UK and Germany (Pear – the World's Biggest Social Experiment, n.d.). To expand my own knowledge of the new emerging dating ideas, I joined that social experiment for single people. It's called Pear Social Experiment, and it costs around $AUD39. The package includes plastic rings that signify being single and ready to mingle so that you can recognize other participants. People from Pear Experiment have access to exclusive events in their cities where single people can roam around and seek romantic connections. Currently there are more men than women participating in the experiment.

I didn't get that much information about Pear events after I purchased the rings. Some of them were advertised online and were not very exclusive, because anyone was able to attend. I have found my current partner through an online app so I stopped waiting for more information from the organisers. I haven't seen many people wearing the rings either. Perhaps this experiment needs more time to kick off properly, improve organisation and reach out to participants more often.

☞ Online Dating Apps

Conducting an internet search when it comes to dating has been on the rise. There are so many available apps on the market that will help you find a suitable person. I used to think that people online don't have enough respect and drive to have a relationship, so why bother. Then I met one of my ex partners on Hinge. My current partner I've also met through Bumble. You can use those platforms in many different ways. There are obviously plenty of scammers and ghosters, but there are also good people. I experienced both nightmare dates, but also had some awesome experiences.

Today, these apps are the most widely studied means of meeting dates. The attitude towards online dating has been evolving over the years. Research conducted in America from 2005 to 2013 has shown some interesting statistics (Smith & Duggan, 2014). At first in 2005 only 44%

of people believed that online dating is a good way to meet people. That number rose to 59% in 2013. Also, 6% more people believe that online dating creates better opportunities to find a better romantic match. In 2005 29% of people believed that online dating is for desperate individuals and in 2013 only 21% reported this opinion. In 2013 11% of adults in America used dating apps or websites to search for a partner. There were slightly more men than women, majority had at least some collage education and were mostly urban living.

The attitude towards online dating used to be more reserved and suspicious. Many people would be looking for an occasional hook up there. As far as my personal experiences went and from what I gathered from my social circles, presumably Tinder got a bad reputation because many people on this platform are looking for meaningless encounters. Perhaps that's why they are trying to turn it around with ads that include some relationship connotations. Let's see if Tinder turns it around.

I wanted to provide you with those statistics to give you hope. If the apps are being perceived as a good platform for finding meaningful and long-term relationships, people will use them for this purpose. I find that the online apps culture has changed for the better.

It's true that online dating is somewhat depersonalized because of lack of initial in-person contact and lack of strings attached. You don't know each other's friends or families and you haven't even seen one another in real life. This makes us feel less accountable for our actions and less connected. But online dating is taking a turn for the better after everything went online in 2019.

If the opinion about online dating is changing for the better, it promotes more respect towards this type of dating, and it can also bring more respectful users. It's currently much more common for people to know couples who met online (Smith & Duggan, 2013). In the early days of swiping in 2005, only 15% of people reported knowing someone who found a relationship or a spouse through online dating platform, while the most recent data shows that in 2013 it was 29%. Logically this will be encouraging others who are in search of something more meaningful and long-term to sign up as well.

Nevertheless, people using online dating platforms can quickly go into a phenomenon that I call rejection mode (Pronk & Denissen, 2019). An increased number of possibilities decreases the probability of making a choice and being satisfied with the choice. We spoke about this phenomenon in Chapter 4 where I pointed out that more options can help us stop idealizing our dates. Because those apps have countless numbers of potential dates, they can lead to wanting more and better options. Have you ever felt that, instead of getting to know your date, you're spending time thinking about scrolling more and finding a better option? Your rejection mode might be kicking in. Researchers explain this occurrence as rejection depletion. When you reject so many people a day by just swiping left, you create an idea in your brain that this action is pointless and therefore tiring and depleting.

Our behavior is driven by trial and error. If we experience "error" or a disappointment because of rejecting a match, we are less likely to perform the same action after many "errors." We've never had so many options when it comes to dating before this century so it's only normal that our brains get confused about this infinite pool of people to reject! When you consider the action to be pointless, you're less likely to be mindful and truly give your dates a go.

Researchers found that we're more likely to accept the people who appear as the first ones during online search (Pronk & Denissen, 2019), that's why apps are earning money from users for letting them appear as the first one in people's swiping list. After the initial excitement hits the mind, the number of right swipes systematically decreases and picks up at the end of the experiment when there are few options left. This was replicated through studying multiple cohorts, that's why the hypothesis is that rejection mode kicks in. If this type of pattern continues for a longtime, people get dating burnout.

Another study has found that merely holding a device in your hand while evaluating potential romantic partners can affect your perception to some degree (Banks et al., 2017). Holding a device decreases perceived attractiveness of the task and the social aspect of the activity. It can also decrease perceived personhood of the individual on the screen, so we tend to dehumanize others more.

To avoid rejection mode or dating burnout you might want to try a different approach. Choose the opposite direction to fatalism. Now that you are aware of rejection mode and dating burnout, use this knowledge to override your automatic brain. Account for your own bias and mindfully choose a different pathway. To do it practically try the exercises below.

* * *

EXERCISE: Mindful Swiping
When you sit down with your dating app keep in mind the information that you just read about online dating. When you look at people's profiles, try to make it personal. Think of them as another human being and not only a photo and a few captions. Thoroughly view their profile, read things that they've written and then make a decision. Do it each time and if you get the urge to swipe through, notice it and continue the exercise. Obviously, there will be some people whom you don't find attractive, but it's more about your approach to the search rather than how quickly you can go through your options.

You don't have to use Mindful Swiping every time. This type of exercise might give you the power to notice your rejection mode. So, if you swipe in your regular way, try to notice the mindless need for rejecting and engage in Mindful Swiping again if you get caught up in automatic behaviors.

* * *

Dating Attitude Check:
Answer the questions below in your journal:
1) Do you find yourself wanting a new match even though you've been texting or seeing someone that caught your attention?
2) Even if you're involved with someone, do you still perceive them as one of the options and catch yourself wondering about who else is out there for you?

3) During a date, do you catch yourself wanting to return to the app and swipe some more instead of getting to know the person in front of you?
4) When you go into a new relationship, are you still waiting for a better match to come along, and keep an eye out just in case?

If you answered "yes" to any of those questions you might be experiencing dating burnout. If this sounds like your pattern, it doesn't look like you're having much fun. You're in a constant state of searching and wanting instead of being and enjoying. Even if you want to date multiple people and you consider this a good mindset to have as a polyam, I will still say it's not very mindful and present. To enjoy dating we need to be in the here and now. Giving people undivided attention means showing respect and give this relation a real try. I encourage you to go back to your inner work and reengage when you are at capacity to date mindfully. Living in a constant state of romantic lack and craving is unhealthy.

When it comes to dating, we might fall into the pit of constantly wanting a new and better partner and we stop enjoying the process itself and the person that is currently in front of us. Wanting and liking are two separate pathways in our brain, even though they sound similar. Wanting something is linked to dopamine which spikes when we get some gratification (Wilson, 2015), for example when you are searching for a new partner and have your hopes up and your head is filled with fantasies about the future. A state of wanting leaves you unfulfilled and hungry for more, we obviously need some of it to keep the excitement in the relationship but if you crave constant novelty with no room for enjoyment, it can become an issue. On the other hand, liking is connected to opioids released by the brain when we're content. This gives us the feeling that we enjoy our situation. Switching to being and enjoying lets you keep stable mental health and decreases the possibility of addictions.

Online Dating Tips:
This advice is based on reading studies on online dating in addition to my own observations and experiences.

GENERAL RECCOMENDATIONS:

1) Dating apps are the busiest around the holidays. This is correlated with the fact that we're reminded about the importance of family because of gatherings that take place during these times of the year. Also, if you're the only single person at a family dinner, it can get confronting and lonely. Hands up, who else was pressured by their moms or aunties about having kids and finding a partner? This phenomenon also means that there will be more new people on the apps who usually might not make an appearance, and some will be driven by a want of a relationship rather than a hook up.

2) Make sure that it's easy to recognize you. If you post only group photos, most people won't sit there to find Wally.

3) Don't catfish! Catfishing is pretending to be someone you're not by using their photos or when you post photos from years ago where you looked very different. You're not only wasting the other person's time but your own as well and creating an uncomfortable situation. There is also plenty of scammers that are after your money and might offer you bitcoin investments or other "opportunities". If someone is talking about such things in the first months of the relation it can be a red flag waving at you.

4) Make sure that your photos are of good quality and that you show your face and body as well. Silhouettes make a massive difference to some people and, as I said, you want to show yourself the way you are, obviously in a good light but if you're faking, it will come out later.

5) Don't be afraid to show your achievements. If you have a graduation photo or one of you winning a trophy, let people know that you have a passion and you are proud of your achievements. That doesn't mean you should brag and bring it up during every conversation.

6) If you want an exciting relationship, you need to be an exciting person. Show a potential date that you have plenty of things going for you, hobbies and that you're fun to be around. Following that logic, if you're looking for something other than excitement you need to

manifest that as well. If you seek a levelheaded and stable person, you need to show yourself as such an individual.

Before you create or remake your profile go back to your "Ideal Partner List" and your "We are All Equal Here" exercise. If you have a realistic idea about who you want as partner, consider if they would find your profile appealing. Try to really put yourself in their shoes. Think of their values, hobbies and what this person could be looking for. For example, if you're looking for a guy who wants to settle down and is loyal, he'll probably not be into partying every night and having a hangover everyday (a wild guess!). So, if you only post photos from binge drinking excursions (I'm Polish so no judgement), then your key audience might skip your profile or come to the date thinking that it will be just a fun drinking date. In an ideal world we're open-minded, but that's not realistic. People work with cues, stereotypes, and impressions. So, try to give the right cues to people that you want to meet. Going back to the example, your alternative can be posting one photo from a party so that your date knows that you enjoy that side of life but add some extra information or photos showing your various interests so they can't "put you in a box". The more variety, the more mystery, and the more mystery, the more interest.

7) Talk about what you want in a partner. If you talk only about your dislikes, it shows other people that there could be some bitterness from past relationships. Talking about positive qualities and your needs shows that you have good boundaries, and you know what you want.

8) It's good to have a phone chat with your online date before you meet them. Voice makes a big difference; you can perhaps get a glimpse of how the conversation will look. You might also find out about their temperament and sense of humor. Also, if someone is devoting their time like this it could indicate that they're serious about meeting you.

9) Be patient with your match's response time. Many people don't have notifications from these apps turned on or are rarely checking them. You might be better off exchanging numbers or social media. Also, remember that you're still strangers, so you will be in a different "category" until you become more familiar. For example, my response

time varies depending on the immediacy of the situation and who is texting me.
10) Keep it short and fun when it comes to profile descriptions and messages. I find that the majority of people on the apps prefer that, so leave the debates for the in-person meeting. But if your match seems to like long paragraphs, you can match their energy!

FOR MEN

1) Upload as many photos of you as you can. Don't waste this space for photos of landscapes, your cars, or memes. I sometimes see very handsome men with only one or two photos, and I swipe left as I don't see any more information. Women like to see that you have an interesting life where you do something, work towards something and value growth. So, choose some hobby, travel, sporty or hiking shots. Perhaps you are into art, books, or music. Take a photo of you in front of your private book or record collection! Show your potential date your true self. Social photos with a couple of friends are also recommended.
2) I'm not sure about others, but for me and women that I interviewed for this book, the bio and captions matter, so guys put some effort there. If there is only one word, I'll imagine monosyllabic conversations.
3) Fill in other information like your height. I know it's somewhat superficial, but height matters in contemporary dating and it's better not to waste time by listing yours. Plenty of apps also let you answer questions like: what are you looking for in terms of relationships? What are your religious or spiritual beliefs? Do you smoke? Do you drink? It's good to answer at least some of them. For some people smoking or drinking can be a deal breaker. The more information you include the better.

FOR WOMEN

1) Ladies! Make sure that you're the spotlight in every photo. From my personal surveys conducted with men, I found out that a lot of them pay more attention to photos than anything written on the profile.

2) Don't wait around for a guy to invite you out. I know there's a strong pull towards passivity to see if the other person is truly interested in you, but you could be wasting your time if you've been texting with this person for a few weeks and there's still no invitation on the horizon. My advice is to give it a week of consistent texting and offer to meet up. Then you can see if your match is taking the initiative, if they're keen or vague about setting up a meeting. You will quickly discover their intentions and then you can truly establish if this relation is worth pursuing.

3) Be safe when it comes to meeting people. Make sure you get to know them a bit better before you meet your match. A good idea is to exchange social media to have a glimpse into their life. Meet in a public place the first time you see them. Another thing that you could do is to let your friend, or a family member know your location.

This is obviously classic advice and there are plenty of exceptions to the rule. Personally, I included my graduation photo, me on a scooter traveling throughout Vietnam, a shot with my old travel van, and a couple of photos with friends at events. In my bio I mentioned my profession, Polish roots and that I'm writing this very book.

In my prompts:

"Descendant of Polish royalty, unfortunately not getting golden coins for it." (to avoid comments like "hey, sugar momma")

"Fun fact: I lived in 5 different countries. Also, a good shot."

"Bought a scooter in Vietnam, traveled alone throughout the country. Story is composed of petrol shortages and jumping fences."

If you can make it playful and informative that's all you need. Most profile elements should tell your story and prompt more questions, making it so much easier for the conversation to flow. You don't even have to think of topics because people are already interested and want to ask you more. Things like strange but funny situations, fun facts and past adventures can always make up a cool profile. So, play around, see what works. Pay attention to which photos and prompts get the most likes. Talk about your hobbies, aspirations, life plans. Ask friends for feedback!

Most popular Dating Apps:
1) Eharmony
2) Academic Singles
3) Elite Singles
4) OkCupid
5) Hinge
6) Tinder
7) Mature Dating
8) Singles50 (for singles above 50 years old)
9) Silver Singles
10) Zoosk
11) Bumble
12) Happen
13) Match.com
14) Grinder (for gay and bisexual men)
15) Her (for lesbians and queer people)
16) Coffee Meets Bagel
17) Facebook Dating
18) Badoo
19) Clover Dating
20) Plenty of Fish
21) Feels (TikTok style dating app where you post short videos instead of photos)
22) Kippo (app matches you depending on what games you prefer, targeting gamers)
23) LOLO Dating and Icebreaker Games

This is only the tip of the iceberg. Online dating has been evolving for some time. It's more common not only to date but also be more open to friendships that can evolve from these apps. Interactive games for people and showing each other short videos allow us to get to know our match better and from different perspectives. Personally, I tried a lot of those apps and the most effective for me are Hinge and Bumble.

There are also more specific apps that allow you to find the right type of person for you. If you're into kink and BDSM and want to find someone specifically with those sexual preferences, or are looking for someone practicing the same religion as you, you can use one of those ones:

Kink & BDSM Friendly apps:
1) Fetlife
2) Kinkoo (to meet people with specific fetishes)
3) Whiplr
4) Kink D
5) Kinki (very LGBTQIA+ friendly)
6) Feeld (very Poly friendly)

Apps connecting you with people of the same faith or culture:
1) Christian Connection
2) Christian Mingle
3) ChristianCupid
4) Aisle (for Indians)
5) Shaadi.com (for Indians)
6) Go.muzz.com (for Islamic folk)
7) Salams (Islamic)
8) Arabian Date
9) Spiritualsingles.com.au
 (for Buddhist and spiritual folk)
10) Jdate (for Jewish people)

There are also apps and websites that you can visit to find someone that just wants to hook up or date casually like AdultFriendFinder. There is even an app that allows you to connect to COVID-19 unvaccinated people because that's their life choice and they seek a likeminded partner. It's called Pure Match. The more specific you can make your search, the more compatible people you can find.

SUMMARY

This chapter discusses various ways in which you can meet your potential dates. We went through a direct approach, which can be difficult for some people but very good for your social skills. Next, I outlined third-party involvement options for meeting dates such as blind dates, speed dating, matrimonial agencies, and new ideas like social experiments. In the last but very substantial part of this chapter, I discussed online dating app realities and provided you with some tips when it comes to creating your online profile and general etiquette on the online dating apps. I have also provided you with a list of different apps that enable you to narrow your search when it comes to your interests, sexual preferences, or religion.

Chapter 12:
Masters of Pickup

This chapter will be devoted to consent and skills surrounding initial contact with your chosen potential partner. Maybe you already noticed a theme where I try to convince you to be a nice human being? I believe that asking someone out requires courage and putting yourself out there to be judged by another people, so I really want to congratulate you. But while picking someone up, we also need to remember other people's boundaries, personal space, and common decency.

We know that men on average have more issues with intrusive behaviors such as sending unwanted sexually explicit messages or stalking (Hess & Flores, 2016; Mayshak et al., 2020). The reporting could be due to the fact that being stalked by a women can seem harmless to men or shameful to report. I was stalked a few times and it's not a great feeling. Most intrusive behaviors will go unreported which does not give anyone permission to indulge in them. Even though these behaviors are more prominent in men, some women engage in them. One of my friends experienced a girl grabbing his penis and making some sexual comments at the same time. Be respectful when it comes to initial contact with others.

I experienced many more of less forward approaches from men. The one that stood out the most happened at a club. Someone offered me a drink and we had a conversation, nevertheless then I decided that I want to rejoin my friends but he was very persistent when it came to staying around me and getting my number. Guys, if a woman wants to leave, let her. You can ask for her number but if you meet even slight resistance, you need to accept defeat. If you press on you might be putting her in a very uncomfortable position especially if she has a people pleasing Part. When this situation happened I was in my early twenties and my boundaries were not as firm as they are now. I tried to leave this person without being very direct and he just kept following me, he also became my stalker. He appeared at my house, apparently knew one of my housemates and then he approached me at the bus where I eventually told him to go away in much harsher words I must admit. This taught me that I need to be more explicit about my needs. These days I'm quite comfortable to say to a man that didn't get my subtle cues that "I'm sorry but I'm not interested, I'm gonna go now."

Subtle approach to asking people out works well, as the fact that we're prone to be interested in scarcity and perceived unavailability. If you strike up a casual conversation, chances are that the person that is interested in you will want to continue to talk to you or will reach out by themselves later if you are, for example, at the same bar or a restaurant. If they don't come back, you can always casually reach out to them with a slightly bigger move for example:" I thought maybe we could exchange numbers before my fiends and I leave?" You need to pay attention to see if that person hasn't left the venue or leave it to fate! It really depends how much you want to see them again.

Pickup lines have become a new sport. You can find endless ideas online. But let me give you some suggestions from my general knowledge, experience, and some hypothetical scenarios:

1) General "How are you doing?" scenario. You don't need to talk about literature when you first meet. Small talk can be a way to go, simple, non-invasive questions can give your potential date a moment to assess your attractiveness and whether he or she is interested.
2) Bring their attention to something or someone in the venue. Maybe not the lighting, but something thought-provoking that captures your attention.
3) Ask for a simple favor like giving directions. You can start a conversation from there or come back later because you've already created

an opening. Make sure you introduce yourself and thank them for the favor.
4) When you're out, make a bet with your friend that you'll speak to or ask someone on a date. You create accountability and more motivation to approach someone if your friend will give you hell for chickening out. You can also tell that potential date that it was a dare if you don't have any other ideas for an opening line at that time. I went out on a couple of dates with a person who used this approach.
5) Approach a group with one of your friends to single out a person that you fancy. Merging two groups gives the vibe of casual and entertainment-seeking behavior. People sometimes just want to mingle. I must add that the ease with which you can casually approach groups is culturally determined. In Australia, or at least in Sydney, it's less common to spontaneously approach people, whereas in Europe it's very common.
6) Asking someone to dance. It's a non-invasive request but it works only if you encounter a confident enough person. Mostly used by men in my experience, perhaps because it's easy to get rejected. If the initial contact is already made and you've had a conversation with that person, they might be more prone to say yes, as they'll feel more comfortable with you.
7) Complimenting someone and directly expressing your interest. Again, it's mostly done by men, but I have seen women doing it very confidently as well. I'll get stereotypical here, but it's just an observation rather than a rule. It seems to me like men can get away with full-blown flattery and displays of strong attraction but women less so. When a woman approaches a man, the message can be taken as "she must be sexually interested; I don't have to try hard". Whereas women would need to add a certain amount of nonchalance and be highly confident for it to work in a way: "wow, she seems great and knows what she wants." If you show an interest but act very confidently and have "not a big deal" type of attitude, people might get confused and therefore more mesmerized by your confidence.

***

Times are changing, and it's more acceptable to express out right interest for both men and women. If you're a reader from the new generation, people would not be surprised that you're willing to approach people for their number. Countless videos on TikTok got very popular just by showing direct questions like: "Do you want to give me your number?". Recently I saw a challenge where a girl easily gathered boys' phone numbers without saying a word. That leads me to believe that each generation has its own code of conduct.

Showing outright that you fancy someone can be vulnerable and you automatically open yourself up to rejection. But if you know you can take rejection gracefully, it can be used as a magnet instead of a repellant. You can show strength of character, honesty and confidence at the same time and a combination of good and appealing character traits is what makes you different. If you can exhibit at least two characteristics that often don't go together, you're ahead of the game but those need to be your prominent traits. For example, funny and book smart; or ambitious and emotionally intelligent; or social butterfly and a stable, loyal partner. If you can do a few good things at the same time, you have double the advantage.

Try to show your best qualities in the initial contact but remember to be mindful of consent and not to go too far. Perhaps your strength is being affectionate, but you can't be very affectionate when you just meet a person. Most of the time, men will have an upper hand physically and that's just biology. Guys make sure that you make a girl feel comfortable and safe. You don't want her to make a decision under pressure. Don't corner her in some creepy spot and keep an adequate distance at first; she doesn't know that you want to take her out just yet. If you find initial contact confronting, use more indirect forms like striking up a casual conversation, meeting dates through friends and family or going for online dating. Nevertheless, try to go out of your comfort zone as much as you can, as it enhances confidence and social skills.

Also, remember that I'm speaking from the perspective of a Millennial. Times are changing quickly, and the dating world gets more liberal. So, make sure to make a note of current trends within your friend's group and dating pool. Try different approaches. The success rate of positive responses to your charms will also depend on the type of people you encounter. Some will be intimidated or weirded out by a direct approach and others will embrace it and think of it highly and as a sign of courage. So don't give up after one or two rejections.

Online Courting

It's important that you can flirt and hold a conversation over a text message. Current society also prefers text messages over a phone call, or a voice note. I find that it's due to an increase in social anxiety and lack of courage to speak, especially, to newly met people. Phone call is more personal and can tell you more about your date.

When you begin a conversation with a new person, you need to ask questions. It's not enough to pay a compliment or say "hey." From experience I can tell you that most of your online matches won't respond or they'll respond once and disappear. I assume the majority has more important things to do; maybe they matched with you by accident, or they changed their mind. Whatever the reason is, the internet provides so much anonymity that often people don't bother responding to messages.

That is why I often choose a simple "Hey! How's it going?". If your match responds, you can continue with more specific questions. Nevertheless, if you are more motivated, it's good to start off with a unique and specific question straight of the bat. Review your match's profile and see what a potential conversational topic could be. Perhaps you can see in the photos that they play an instrument or are reading a specific book. Ask them about it. If you see that you have some interests in common, tell them about it; this could be a great opportunity to bond with your match.

Many women wait for men to contact them, but you don't have to do that. I really enjoy the Bumble dating app because women must send the first message. This pushes me to take action. If you don't create an opportunity for others to reach out to you, you won't have as many options. When you start chatting for a bit longer you need to start thinking about asking the other person out.

For me a rule of thumb is one or maximum two weeks of texting and after that I would expect an invitation or invite my match out myself. If I don't see the invitation coming from the man, I might ask them out if the conversation is flowing and they seem interested. I wouldn't bother with someone who is resurfacing every week or so and hasn't made any plans to see me. You can travel in circles for weeks only to discover you've wasted your time.

Also, be respectful. The online world grants us anonymity, but often people will abuse that to make other people feel bad or to get sexually excited. So don't send any unwanted sexually explicit photos or make sleazy comments. People don't appreciate being treated like objects. Remember, on the other side is a person with feelings, thoughts, dreams, goals, family, and friends.

Other than that, try to keep it nice and simple. Make jokes and try to find out more about your match. If both of you want to talk about deep and difficult things straight away that's great, but perhaps parts of the conversation will get lost in translation. Sometimes it's better to wait with big debates until you meet, so that you don't misinterpret anything.

If some phrase that your match texted seems weird to you, don't be afraid to ask about it or if you can see that your match is not following the thread of your thought bring it up as well. I was texting with my current partner after a second date and I wanted to flirt with him a bit by asking him to step into a role of my personal trainer that needs to give me some incentives for being good and consistent with my efforts. He continued with being professional about it and didn't know what to offer but a Coke Zero. I chose to admit that it was a flirting attempt and that I would prefer a kiss such as the one we've had at the end of our dates. We had a good laugh about it during our third date and that definitely prompted more kissing.

Now that you're aware of different ways to meet your potential dates, you can focus on practicing. The following exercise provides structure to your search and an opportunity to enhance your social and dating skills.

* * *

EXERCISE: Initial Contact & Pick-Up Skills
Use small steps just like in the exercises from Part 1 Chapter 8: Social Skills Curriculum. Each week or fortnight set up a small achievable goal when it comes to dating. Here are some potential situations that you might find yourself in and some ideas for commitments.

If you don't have any dates lined up start to make commitments such as:

- Make a commitment to initiate a conversation with two people who you find attractive, per week.
- Make a weekly commitment to invite one person on a date. It counts regardless of the outcome.
- Make a commitment to flirt with three people whom you find attractive in one week. It can be a random person on a train that you strike up a conversation with.
- Experiment with different approaches to initiation, as discussed in the previous chapter.
- Each time you approach a prospective date, try to come up with a slightly different way of starting the conversation. Make a note of what worked and what didn't and what could be improved next time.
- Experiment with settings when you initiate conversations with potential dates. Try different places and situations. Make a mental note of which one felt most comfortable and why.

* * *

SUMMARY
In this chapter I presented you with various ways to ask out your date. We talked about the importance of consent and making the other person feel

comfortable to say "yes" to a date but also to be able to say "no." I presented you with some pick-up ideas that you can use and practice. Create your own ideas as well; people will often appreciate original opening lines. It can show your ingenuity and creativity. We also spoke about the importance of confidence when it comes to approaching someone. In addition, we discussed online pickup and conversations. Lastly, at the end of the chapter, I provided an exercise to help you practice your social skills when it comes to making initial contact with potential dates. I hope all the tips and suggestions will help you to navigate online dating confidently.

Chapter 13:
Dating Social Skills Curriculum

In this chapter we discuss various social skills that are needed for romantic interactions such as emotion, interpersonal, and intrapersonal intelligence. We also discuss how to share and reciprocate energy with others so that you create deep and fulfilling connections. I'll provide you with some tips and ideas that will help you practice your interpersonal skills. We will delve into different conversation topics that you can bring up, joking, and various types of flirting. This should give you a deeper understanding of what it means to skillfully connect to others.

Social skills include emotional intelligence, which means being able to read other people's emotions and also to acknowledge your own emotional world. When you're able to do it, you can choose your words and actions in a way that doesn't hurt you or the other person, and you can also understand others and yourself much better. Having good social skills also means to have good communication in general, and to stay composed and connected even when you're talking about difficult topics. We also need to be able to "read the room," which means to acknowledge our surroundings and the people who are around us. We need to act in a way that's appropriate for a given situation so we should be aware of social norms and rules. Another important side of social interactions is reading other people's boundaries and creating your own. For this you will not only need emotional and interpersonal intelligence but also intrapersonal understanding. We already know that to form good boundaries we need introspection and harmonious inner dialogue.

Communication, relationships, and connection are all about the exchange of energy. We all give off some type of "vibe." If you're angry, aggressive, or annoyed, you're giving off negative energy. When you're happy, fulfilled, and cheerful, you can share positive energy with others. To share the positivity, you can be curious about your date and their interests, get excited with them, ask insightful questions, pay them a compliment, or entertain them with a joke. All of this creates connection from your side. But for the connection to be complete, your date needs to reciprocate and match this positive energy. Someone that gives off only the negative will bring you down and deplete you very quickly.

Of course, we should be able share the negative energy as well if your date is having a hard time. Nevertheless, if you just met, your connection isn't strong enough to withhold massive amounts of negativity. Difficult emotions need to be balanced with a positive connection. A long-term relationship already has love and commitment to balance the negativity. So, remember that your initial communication should be mainly on the light and positive side.

To become a true master of initiating contact with others and also dating and relationships, you need to start practicing skills that you already have and build on them. You most likely bought this book because what you were doing in the past wasn't effective. Doing something over and over again and expecting different outcomes is in fact a definition of insanity. So let me show you a new way. You already have some social skills, but we learn more throughout our lives. Dating comes much later than our general social interactions. To practice your dating skills, you need more exposure. If you have a date or dates lined up and want to expand your skills here are some ideas for you.

1. Experiment with types of dates
Experiment with different types of dates like meeting at a bar, at a restaurant, cafe, art gallery or participating in a sports activity. See which type suits you best and what type of environment you feel most comfortable with. At the end of every date, think of the pros and cons. Consider how

it felt and the level of connection with your date. Did it increase or decrease? You can even ask your date for feedback on how they liked the settings and why.

I find that men tend to have more activity-focused friendships whereas women prefer the relationship itself and conversations instead of an activity or a hobby that they perform with their friends. That's why often on dates men would bond more through doing things together and women through conversations. This is a broad spectrum rather than a rule. By incorporating both deep conversations and activities, you can make sure that both of you can bond in the best way possible.

2. Create a List of Topics

Come up with a list of topics suitable for a date that you enjoy talking about. Test each topic mindfully and think what it makes you feel when you talk about each one. Does your date engage in it or not? Even if you see less engagement, don't get discouraged; some people simply aren't interested in certain subjects. Nevertheless, if you're testing one of the topics for the tenth time and it goes downhill each attempt, perhaps it's not the best topic for the first date or you need a very specific audience for it.

3. Practice Humor

Commit to making at least one or two jokes per date. Your chosen number will depend on your confidence level. If you're already super stressed it's probably not the best idea to overdo it. Ideally, you could organically come up with jokes but, if it's not within your nature, it won't happen magically. Joking is also a social skill that needs to be practiced. The more you do it, the more comfortable you become, and your jokes will improve. It's okay to have scripted jokes on a date. You just met the person so it's doubtful they have heard the joke from you before. Then, you can improve your joke, elaborate on it, and even bring it up again with a different person if it was well received previously. Jokes are an artform that constantly shifts, we can reuse them in different situations and contexts. You'll see how much good feedback (laughter) you get and know if you're on the right track.

We also need to remember to tailor the jokes to our audience; we don't want to be offensive and super edgy, especially on a first date. But you can test your audience too. You can try increasing the edginess and see the reaction. Perhaps you can connect with each other by being edgy and politically incorrect together! Practice this also outside of dates, with your friends and family. Ask for feedback and be open to constructive criticism. The more you practice, the more you can just have fun with it. That's the way standup comedians work. If you don't get a laugh out of your date, you could still turn it around. You can acknowledge that you tried to make a joke, but it didn't work out for example, by saying with a confident and nonchalant smile on your face: "No? Nothing? That didn't work out, hey! I'll do a better one next time!" It shows your audience that you experiment like this often, so you're not offended. It deescalates the situation and clears the air.

Being funny can massively add not only to your personality but your general sex appeal. Statistically women think of men as funny and appealing when they tell good jokes and make them laugh. Whereas men usually think of women as funny and appealing when their date laughs at their joke. Only men seem significantly more appealing when they're funny in women's eyes. Despite the above finding, I believe we girls can positively stand out as well when we're quick witted. The evidence is unclear on whether one sex is funnier than the other. The stereotype is that men are funnier, and one study has found that both men and women tend to prefer jokes made by men (Bressler & Balshine, 2006). Nevertheless, we can't be sure if this was due to the jokes themselves or bias. If the pair of you can easily bounce jokes off each other and have amazing banter, connection comes easily.

The Gottman Institute also found that couples who use humor as a de-escalation mechanism after a fight are more likely to stay together (Gottman et al., 1998). So, jokes are your remedy and glue that keep you close. Jokes can also go very well together with flirting. You can convey a lot of sexual tension under the cover of flirtatious jokes. It mixes with teasing and playfully luring your date closer to you.

Think of your Perfect Partner List. Did you put the usual: attractive, smart, funny? Those are the most common traits that people mention while imagining their future partner, if you can master jokes, you have one third figured out.

Become a Skilled Flirt

Flirting is very important when it comes to dating skills. We need to let our date know that we're romantically interested or at least be able to respond to romantic cues if our date displays them. You can flirt in many ways--physically, verbally, and non-verbally. Here are the explanations of each type and some ideas for you to try.

☞ Physical:

For this, you will need to establish your date's personal space boundaries. Playful and casual touch on a hand can be your anchor, most people will not have an issue with it on a date but pay attention to your date's reaction or ask them if it's okay to touch them. From there, you can either wait for your date's move or check other forms of noninvasive touch like a slight and quick touch on a knee or a shoulder when you explain something. Keep checking your date's reaction to make sure you're not invading their personal space. You can progress the touch with your date's permission and depending on the quantity and quality of the dates that you have already had together.

Make sure that you keep track of what is okay with both of you. For some people a passionate kiss on a first date is a "hell, yes!" and for others "maybe next time." It can also depend on the length of the date and strength of the connection that you've created already. If you've had an hour coffee date, it can be too early for some people. But if you've spent a few hours talking and vibing, maybe you both feel up for it.

Some Physical Flirting Ideas:
- When you establish rough idea about your date's personal space you can ask them if you can fix their hair slightly if it seems to be out of place. Or if you believe that your date will be okay with it, playfully and lightly move their hair for no apparent reason or add a compliment.

- Switch your position so that your body is directed towards them or decrease the distance slightly and see your date's reaction.
- Lightly touch their shoulder or knee when you explain something. If you do it during a pause, it can seem too intense. If they keep their attention on the conversation and seem at ease, that's a good sign. However, if they track your hand with their eyes and seem uneasy, it's a cue to back up.
- Offer to read their palms even if you know nothing about it. You can make up a story and have a laugh about it. It will be obvious that the touch and the joke were more important than the actual reading. You can run your fingers through their palms slowly and create some tension. Make sure that they're having fun each step of the way.
- Playfully ask to compare the size of your hands by putting them together. You can then also get curious about your date's hand and give them a compliment. Simple touch can elicit a lot of pleasure as well, if done intentionally and with consent.
- Ask them to compare your height too. It's a playful activity where you can lean against each other.
- Ask if they have any tattoos. That can sometimes create another opportunity for flirtatious touch and questions about the artwork.

☞ Verbal:

Verbal cues can be composed of a sense of challenge, teasing, playfulness, and compliments. Think of verbal flirting as a balance of humor and sexual tension. You don't want to be very obvious and explicit with your desires and praise at the beginning but try to build it up as the date goes on. This also applies in online flirting.

Some Verbal Flirtation Ideas:
- Crafty compliments like: "You look like you could do a few squats with me on your shoulders" (girl to a guy) add slight tough on the arm or even squeeze his biceps.
- If you forgot what to say you can always come back with "Your eyes are so distracting I got lost there for a second. What was I saying?".

Simple honest compliments do the job as well. If you think it's a bit cheesy, it probably is because first dates should be cute like this. There is a level of innocence in those first encounters, so if you can do cute and cheesy things confidently you are ahead of the game.
- Playful acknowledgement and interpretation of your date's actions and words. If your date does something that makes you think that they like you, bring it up. E.g., "Seems to me like you can't take your eyes off me. Hmm?". You're not only playful but also planting an idea in their head that they like you and think about you.
- Talking about the way your date makes you feel like. E.g., "Oh, I just love how you open the door for me every time. Such a gentlemen. You make me feel like a princess." or "I liked when you leaned on me when we were doing that walk in the park today." Leave the most vulnerable disclosures for later but try to experiment with showing your feelings bit by bit. You will also show yourself as a person who knows what he or she wants and is not afraid to reinforce and compliment behaviors in others.
- Trying to ask increasingly suggestive questions. When you establish some trust and closeness, suggest playing 20 questions or truth or dare. Be sure to check if your date is comfortable with it. It can also increase your much needed knowledge about your date's preferences when it comes to life, relationships, and intimacy, so make mental notes. If you both giggle and blush at the end of every question you're doing it right!

☞ Non-verbal:
Simply looking at each other and gestures can be flirty as well. If someone is interested in you, they will scan your face from side to side and will be also focusing on your mouth. We also tend to play with our hair and prolong the time we gaze at the person that we're attracted to. We can also focus on the rest of the body of our date. If you're visibly pleased when your date is walking towards you, she or he can also tell that you like what you see. So, make it apparent that you enjoy the view by smiling and

perhaps adding a verbal compliment! From a study done by Kellerman et al. (1989) we know that prolonged gazing at the other person brings in feelings of affection and love for strangers.

Some Non-Verbal Flirtation Ideas:
- Lingering gaze. You obviously don't want to stare, but if your date is giggling and generally pleased with prolonged gazing, use it to flirt with them. Silence doesn't have to be awkward. If you just finished a fun topic and ended up just looking at each other with pleasure in your eyes and smiling, stay like this for a bit and see what their reaction will be. You can even look down for a little bit and come back with your gaze. If you see that they just did the same thing there can be a joint sense of tension and longing because it seems like it's hard for both of you to stop looking at each other. When we're attracted to someone, we have a strong need to look at them as often as we can.
- Smiling. Try using different types of smiles and see which one gets you the most attention and reciprocation.

SUMMARY

In this chapter I talked about social skills in the context of romantic relationships and dating. With the help of this book, you hopefully already practiced your general social skills. Nevertheless, romantic connections are more complex. That is why in this chapter I've outlined to you how to create a deep and meaningful connection with someone. We discussed emotional, interpersonal, and intrapersonal intelligence that is needed for connection building. We also talked about sharing and reciprocating energy with other people. Lastly, I've given you some tips on picking topics of conversations, skillfully joking and flirting. Joking, flirting, and conversing are skills that need to be practiced, you need ideas, feedback, and time to truly master it. Exposure is the only way!

Chapter 14:
First Date and Early Stages

In this chapter, we discuss a few topics that are very important for the early dating stages. We discuss planning initial dates when it comes to the setting and length of meetings. You obviously want to introduce your date to your life in steps, in order to not overwhelm them. Next, we delve into subjects you might want to discuss during dates. Lastly, we talk about a very controversial question which is "Who should pay on a date?" You can analyze different opinions and facts when it comes to gender pay gap, and biological and social differences between men and women.

Planning Initial Dates

The environment for a first date is important. If you initiated the meeting, you should consider a few different options. The most common places are bars, restaurants, or cafes. Everyone needs to eat and drink, so it's an obvious joint activity. It's probably the safest option, but make sure that your date is happy with the place. You don't want to push for a surprise and find out that you invited a newly recovering alcoholic to a bar for instance. Just to be on the safe side, make sure that you're both on the same page when it comes to activities.

    Speaking of alcohol on dates. Should you be drinking? And if so, how much? Obviously, alcohol can nicely loosen you up, so you don't feel as much social pressure, but drinking impedes your ability to read red flags and social cues properly. There is a fine line between fun drunk and unappealing drunk so be aware where your line and limitations are. Your date just met you, he or she doesn't know how great you are; they only see how drunk and uncommunicative you got right there. Also, if you need to be intoxicated to have fun with that person, it's not the best sign. You won't be able to truly say if you fit together until you can enjoy each other's company while sober. You also don't show who you really are as a person, but a version of you that had one too many.

For people who have a hard time gathering their thoughts and conversing on a first date, choose a fun activity instead. This also prevents you from overdrinking. Both you and your date will be occupied with an activity. Make sure you don't choose a cinema or theatre where you can't really talk for a couple of hours. It can be a good idea in the future when you know each other better. Here are some suggestions: book mini-golf, go-carts, bowling, a boat tour or go to an amusement park. You can also ask your date for an opinion. Everyone has a different way of bonding and prefers certain environments to others, so your date's answer provides more information about how to best create a connection with them.

If you enjoy sports and you know that your date does too, you can teach each other something. If you' play golf, boxing, or do yoga, you can set up an active date and show your partner the ins and outs of your hobby. You can even include some healthy competition. I emphasize healthy, because if it's not, your date can switch from memorable to toxic very quickly. From my experience, it's no fun when your date pushes you to the limit physically and makes fun of you if you can't match their pace or body image idea. Make sure that you make it a joint activity and match your date's slower pace. If they surprise you, however, and beat you at your own game, take it humbly. No one likes a sore loser, especially on a date. A good partner can be happy for their significant other, even if it happens that they lose, and it stings a bit.

NOT First Date Ideas:

☞ At Home
It can be a bit confronting to visit someone at their house if you don't know much about them. Especially if you're a woman invited by a man,

unless it's purely casual arrangements and both of you are happy with that. Even if that is the case, it could still be nice to meet in a public place somewhere, get comfortable with each other and then proceed to the bedroom. But if casual is not your style, it's best to meet in a public place until you feel more comfortable with your date.

☞ With Friends
It's a bold move to invite your date to hang out with your friends. You can easily intimidate your date and your friends at the same time. The first date should be the time for the two of you to get to know each other. Even on the third date you can "violently" find out that your romantic interest is an unapologetic hardcore techno lover who will force his favorite music on you and your friends to the point that you just want to escape.

☞ Getaways
A day trip can be a nice thing, but an overnight stay can be a bad idea for a first date. Even a day trip can be a bit confronting if you've only just met someone. Give yourself the opportunity to get to know the other person and have a bit of time to contemplate if you want to continue seeing them before inviting them on a longer excursion. Of course, sometimes you meet a person with whom there is no end to a conversation. But if that's not the case, it doesn't always mean you won't be good together. People get shy and nervous on dates, when you run out of generic topics it can be hard to gather your thoughts. If you end up not talking and still have half a day ahead of you it may seem like you're not a good fit. When perhaps you are just not that comfortable together yet.

* * *

Pick your settings and environment wisely. Keep it nice and short in the beginning if you want to play it safe. If, on the other hand, you welcome the unexpected, you can progress more quickly to longer and more complex meetings such as including your friends when you meet. Putting your date in those situations will tell you a lot about them. If you only keep it cute, short, and secluded, you're probably missing out on a lot of inside information, and green but also red flags that might also go unnoticed. You don't truly know a person until you see how they interact with your family and friends. You need to see that they make an effort to interact with them in a positive way. Longer trips will also help you establish whether you can spend more time in each other's company. If you keep it shallow, you might be creating a Fairy Tale instead of a relationship. Personally, I'm quite curious when it comes to new people, and I was never afraid to get burned so after the initial couple of dates I was happy to introduce my romantic interest to my friends.

* * *

First Date Topics
Whether you like it or not, conversation is a vital part of a date. We already went through various social skills needed but let's talk about specific topics that frequently come up on dates.

☞ Obviously one of them is work. This question will come up at some point whether you like it or not. Even if you hate your job, it's good to have an answer ready. If it's a super boring position, you can jokingly make it very fascinating. If you're unhappy with what you do, consider talking about your passion or a future plan. Perhaps you're in a transition period and are on the way to a new career. Mention it to your date and focus on it instead of your current position. Nevertheless, if you hate what you do and you don't think about changing it, it can't be a healthy thing for you. Perhaps there are circumstances that are holding you back from action, but you can talk about your dreams as well. If you're passionate about what you do, let the other person know what's so amazing about your profession. What's truly appealing to people is our drive, motivation, and passion for things. If you're not passionate about anything at all, your date may conclude that you won't be passionate about a prospective relationship either and we all want someone motivated and willing to work with us.

☞ Hobbies and interests usually follow as the most popular topic. That's why it's so important to discover what you like to do in life. If all that you do is sit at home and watch TV, you can't be surprised that you can't find a unique and exciting partner. So put some effort into self-development and having new experiences that promote it. It's a great substitute if you're still in a job that you don't like. Make this your subject for displays of passion and motivation.

☞ Family is also one of the more common topics. Obviously, you don't want to tell your date all your childhood traumas the first or second time you see them. This creates the impression that you are seeking a free counselling session. Nevertheless, there's always space for some funny stories from childhood or some more non-invasive family history. If there were some unpleasant experiences, you can mention them in passing if you've healed from them mostly. Maybe you took away an important lesson from hardship. Vulnerability in the right amount can be really good for connection, even at the beginning stage of dating.

As a therapist I have always asked some questions about childhood. That's what made us. Even if you meet someone that only looks towards the future and thinks they're unaffected by the past and uninterested in yours, you can rest assured that they too have some behavioral patterns created by parents. Main communication patterns usually come from childhood. Some behavioral patterns can also be developed by romantic relationships, but the foundation will come from primary caregivers or will be created as a response to a primary caregiver. Before committing, I strongly suggest some conversations about your respective families. If there's no way for you to get anything out of your date when it comes to this topic it could be a potential red flag. It's okay not to share in the beginning, but if he or she wants a relationship and labels, you need this information to make the right choice for yourself instead of going in blindly.

☞ Hopes for the future can also be a fun topic, even for a first date. I'm not talking about hopes and dreams for the relationship with that particular date. Everyone has some sort of idea about their future direction. If you stay hypothetical, there's no reason to hide your needs and wants. It's even fine to say that you want a committed relationship with someone in the future. If you phrase it right, it will not pressure your date. In fact, a person who is terrified of commitment and who pretends to be interested in you and just wants to have some fun will probably get discouraged and might stop wasting your time earlier. That gives you more time to find a person who is unafraid of what you want. Your hopes and dreams can be related to other things in your life as well such as travelling, career, experiences, knowledge, courses, or lifestyle changes.

People are often afraid that they'll come off as too forward and scare the date off. As long as you're not asking them to marry you and you're not proclaiming your love for them, it's acceptable to be honest about what you want in life in general. If you decided to say, "I'm open to any type of relationship" while in your soul you know you lied to seem more chilled and laid back, you're not doing yourself any favors. If your date is counting on a casual relationship and you're secretly hoping for commitment, both of you are going in under false pretense.

By saying "I want a committed relationship down the track but I'm happy to explore for now" you let your date know that you know what you want but you're still in the exploration stage. You're not trying to pressure anyone into a relationship but in that moment, they find out that if at some point it's not going to be with them you will find someone that will commit. I believe that your love interest, whether on a first date or 20 years into a relationship, should be aware that you can leave the relationship. It's our biggest leverage that prevents us from getting too comfortable and therefore lose interest in our date or a partner. Knowing that you can leave at any point and have strength to do it lets you and your partner or a date choose each other each and every day.

☞ Sharing opinions and thoughts is another type of connection. Current world events, science, spirituality, religion, and social views can make up a great conversation if you like a debate and a challenge. It can prompt a conversation about your general outlook on life and the world. Remember to be open and that not everyone will share your option. This can also make you realize your date's values. If your basic principles and values align with theirs that's the most important thing. Many couples will disagree on topics but will have common values and still be able to get along.

If you're the type of a person who needs to have a partner who shares their particular opinions, you definitely decrease your pool of potential partners. Maybe you need to narrow your search. Perhaps look for dates at specific political or social gatherings where people sharing similar opinions come together. We need to find a partner that has a similar outlook on things like money, preferred family structure, morality and has the same priorities in life.

☞ Habits and day-to-day life can be one of the non-invasive topics for a first date. Even though it may seem unimportant, it can really let you have a glimpse into your date's intimate life. Share your routines and see if anything aligns. Perhaps both of you are coffee drinkers; or both of you like to sing in the shower; or you must hug your pet before you leave for work every day. Small things can bond you as well, especially if it's something quirky and unusual. It can make you feel seen and understood.

All of these types of conversation will result in you sharing your personal experiences, thoughts, emotions, and values, so be prepared to go into each of these aspects during conversations. If you omit emotions, you might fail at creating emotional connection. If you're not sharing your thoughts and knowledge, you might be missing out on intellectual connection. If you don't mention your values, preferred path in life and experiences, your joint path is also not likely to evolve. You need to develop each of those areas to a certain degree.

Who Pays? Female and Male as Biological and Social Constructs

Historically, men paid for everything mainly because they were the ones to have jobs or had better paying jobs than women. Women also have more at stake when it comes to relationships and sex that's why it's common to believe that a man should put in more effort and resources at the beginning of a relationship. If a girl got pregnant with the wrong guy, she was left with an unwanted pregnancy. Men don't have that problem.

The world has changed massively since those days. Contraception is widely available. Abortion is possible in many countries and social support and family courts will get you your money if you choose to keep the child. Discrepancies in earnings are also going down. Women are still earning less on average than men, but it's due to many different factors. The current gender pay gap is largely due to the fact that women tend to choose lower paying jobs that have a better work-life balance (Barbulescu, & Bidwell, 2013). Women are also on average lower on a scale of assertiveness and higher on agreeableness in comparison to men which leads to, for example, a lower rate of women asking for promotions (Judge et al., 2012). Women also tend to work fewer hours on average and take more time off because of pregnancies and maternity leave (Barbulescu, & Bidwell, 2013), although paternity leave is increasingly popular. I don't think it's a bad thing to focus more on your life and family and both women and men should be able to choose their work-life balance. Men who are highly agreeable and choose to focus on other things besides work will also tend to be overlooked for promotions (Judge et al., 2012).

The truth is our bodies and needs are different and we can't skip over that. Biological women have to go through menstruation and if we want to have our own child, we need to be the ones to go through hormonal and body changes tied with pregnancy and are at higher risk of sexually transmitted infections. We also have fewer fertile years than men and our involvement in creating a child is much more complex, therefore women more than men feel pressure to have their lives together earlier. For a very long time in history, we were conditioned to be the nurturers, not the bread winners. The change started to happen in recent decades, and we can't expect that the beliefs and biases will switch immediately.

Men hold most of the wealth in the world, but it's important to add that most of wealth is held by a very tiny percentage of men who are the wealthiest people on the planet. On average most laborers are men, and the majority of homeless and incarcerated people are also men. So, there's a broader spectrum of the gender pay gap than many think (Channel 4 News, 2018). Even so, there was and still is favoritism towards men in several industries, and big cultural differences when it comes to gender roles. In this book we focus on Western societies, however, it's important to acknowledge that in developing countries gender pay gap is a much bigger issue.

I used to want to explain why my Eastern European culture puts so much emphasis on men paying for everything and stopped at gender pay gap. But while researching, I concluded that the gender pay gap is not as significant as it used to be, even though I disagree with the absence of patriarchy, idea put forward by psychologist Jordan Peterson. Time taken to look after a child can affect retirement and is usually utilized by women. Nevertheless, this also comes down to societal expectations. Not only organizational policies need to change but the mind set about child rearing held by the public if we are supposed to see further changes in pay gaps.

The world was first built to accommodate the wants of men before it started to equalize. People were too focused on surviving to be considering how to provide equal opportunities to both sexes. All women knew in life was how to raise kids, cook and keep the house going, not many were keen to leave the familiar. Men always had the biological advantage which comes with physical strength, so they were going into the wild. They were also the first ones to occupy new positions of power. I don't say it was right or wrong. It just was. Now we're a different type of society.

Law is also changing in accordance with societal evolutions. It's illegal to lower the pay of an employee based on their sex. Nevertheless,

I don't discount some toxic work environments that still practice such sexism behind closed doors. I experienced it firsthand. "Men's clubs" are common in many professions, for example DJ work, accounting, or hospitality. And some cultures still favor having boys over girls. It's a slow process, but we're on the right track. It's important to understand those fundamental differences between sexes before going into a debate on "Who should pay on dates?".

However, the fact is Western countries became more egalitarian, so dates become increasingly "equal" when it comes to paying bills. Some people like it, some don't. Some will stick to the "gentlemen era" and some will call for equal rights. I believe it's just a nice thing to do to offer to pay for a woman or perhaps to pay first just as a reminder of the old times and taking the initiative is a manly thing to do in many women's eyes. If you crave strong and traditional male and female energies in your relationship, you need to remember that you are not going to get it if you don't ascribe to your respective role. If you want a traditional relationship as a man, you need to take the initiative, lead, and provide and as a woman you need to look after your partner in an emotional sense and nurture him.

If you are not looking for a traditional union, you will need to redefine the roles and find a partner who will be supportive in other ways and has compatible views when it comes to a relationships. Currently a lot of couples like to be very equal when it comes to the type of contributions they make. I heard opinions from many heterosexual women that couple's life is more beneficial for men. Because majority of household chores and child rearing is done by females who might also be working on top of it. I do encounter a lot of couples who have this dynamic. What is the causality of this occurrence? We can sit here and blame parents, school and TV but the truth is we run our relationships and have choices even if influences around us are strong. If you want to feel equal in both traditional and modern type of relationships you need to negotiate, communicate and discuss. Tailor the relationship to your needs not to the opinions of others. Happiness and fulfillment doesn't just happen to us, we need to make it happen.

We need to remember that everyone was raised in different households and that has massive effects on the way we behave in social situations. Especially if you are, like me, often dating cross culturally. For instance, I was raised in Eastern Europe and the culture there puts a lot of emphasis on guys being chivalrous gentlemen, looking after their woman and paying on dates. Whereas I found Australia focuses on more equality. I didn't know what should be required and expected while dating people from different backgrounds.

I'm not going to say that men should or shouldn't pay for dates. Everyone has their own code of conduct. Nevertheless, it would be nice if both parties offered to pay at some point. I heard so many assumptions about the payment arrangements that you will need to make up your own mind about it. One of my girlfriends doesn't like when a man pays for her because she feels sexually obliged to a degree, whereas my other girlfriends think that a man should always pay. Some men that I interviewed said that if a girl doesn't let them pay on a date, she's definitely not interested in them romantically. Some of my past dates always wanted to pay for me and some wanted to split the bill from the beginning. Another interesting perspective that I heard was: If you invite, you pay.

My favorite story about my late aunt was that she broke off the engagement because her fiancé didn't want to pay an extra PLN50 for her engagement ring. She summed it up with "Sounds like he'll be counting my potatoes in the future." She had a point; you don't want a partner who is constantly looking at the money. If you truly like someone, both of you will feel the need to contribute in some way.

Frankly, I came to the conclusion that I'm happy if a guy pays for the first date or first drinks and, when I get more comfortable, I'll offer to pay myself at some point during the date. So, I guess I'm trying to preserve a bit of my Eastern European upbringing and sprinkle in some consideration and equality. But if it happened that they wanted to split the bill, I of course feel obliged or maybe I just perceived them as less interested or counting my potatoes. Unapologetically, my Polish roots run deep. It's sometimes hard to override the bias.

This made me think about a guy I was dating a while ago. On a first date he wanted to split the bill and he had realized that he ordered more than I did during the dinner. The waitress asked if we want to go item by item or to split 50/50. I just said that 50/50 is fine. I didn't want to count those potatoes. He offered to transfer the rest of the money to me, and said that there is no need. I did go on few more dates with him because we had a good connection but the relation eventually dissolved anyway. There was not enough initiative from his side and I lost interest. One of my ex partners also kept count of our spendings in his mind and I could feel it every time we went to pay. It was rather uncomfortable and made me count things in my mind as well, which I have never done before. But I know that everyone has a different approach and feelings about money. He grew up differently to me and there seemed to be a lot of financial fear surrounding us while going out and that is just something to accept now.

With my current partner there is no such issue. He would be the first one to reach for the wallet after dinner, but then he wouldn't be afraid to tell me if he maxed out his bank account. Even early on in the relationship I would be happy to buy us some more expensive tickets because of his approach to money. Whereas with my ex we would usually count things up and transfer each other the difference. It makes it some much nicer and lighter if both people are not thinking too much about that dollar or two difference.

Nevertheless, when you are getting deeper into the relationship you should have some discussions when it comes to approach to money and running a household to make sure that you are on the same page and everything is running smoothly. If you and your partner have different ideas about investing and building wealth it might be a problem in the future.

Remember that people are just as confused as you about the payment arrangements. Go with the flow. Don't demand people pay for you. The rest you can figure out as you go. If you're unwilling to adjust to another culture perhaps you should stick to dating within your own culture to avoid disappointments. When you are dating someone, it's a good idea to be aware of their cultural norms.

SUMMARY

This chapter was devoted to the early dating stages. We discussed various settings that you can choose for your initial dates and how to gradually introduce your date into your world. I also presented you with some good discussion topics worth exploring before deciding to commit to someone. Lastly, we discussed how the evolving world and society impact current dating trends. I have outlined how our biological differences have created societal division in gender roles, which in turn had a big impact on earnings and job opportunities for both sexes. This discussion was meant to help you analyze different perspectives before deciding "Who should pay on a date?" We went through some common opinions on that subject to help you figure out your own.

Chapter 15:
Intimacy and Sexuality in Early Stages of Dating

This chapter discusses affection, intimacy, and sexuality in the early stages of dating. First, we delve into Love Languages and Styles that allow us to give affection to another person and show our interest through generosity (Chapman, 1992; Seven Love Styles, 2023). We must be able to show our generosity and ability to connect also during this initial dating period. Our Love Style or Language is a unique way in which we prefer to show and receive affection. I outline every one of those Languages and Styles. Next, we explore sexual connectedness in your new relationship. We start with a discussion about the first kiss and when and why it should happen. Then, we move on to sex and discuss what type of mindset you should adopt before making a decision about when and whether to have it. We also talk about the importance of sexual and mental compatibility. Lastly, we will discuss how to break it to your date that you have sexual issues or STIs and how to approach those as a team.

A Word on Generosity and Love Languages
Generosity is a quality that every good partner has. If you want to live your life only thinking about yourself, you're not ready for a committed relationship. People can be generous in many different ways; you don't have to pay every time to prove your generosity. You can also be generous with your time. Make sure the attention that you give is uninterrupted and

undivided. Just because you're together in the same room, it doesn't mean that you're generous with your time. Put your phones away, ask some questions, get curious about the other person, show support if needed.

We can also demonstrate generosity with thoughts. For example, show how much attention you've been paying to your date's conversation. You can bring up points that they've made or organize an activity that they've been wanting to do. It shows how much you think about them.

Touch and words can also be generous. If you know that your date likes to be praised or touched, do it if you feel you have the capacity. Even if it's not the way you usually show affection, it says a lot about your generosity if you do. Being giving means that we're able to show affection and interest in the other person.

This brings us to the idea of Love Languages or Styles. Those are the ways in which we prefer to give and receive love from others, and which are often learned from our parents or primary caregivers. They develop early in life and are consistent throughout our lifetime.

Love Languages can be a nice and non-invasive topic, even for a first date. Ask your date "How do you like to be shown affection?" This can lead you to discuss Love Languages. You can even bring up the whole theory behind Love Languages as a fun fact. Love Languages were the first theory that named and grouped our preference for a certain kind of affection. This idea was created by Dr. Garry Chapman who came up with five main Languages as follows:

1. Quality Time
People who have this Love Language enjoy undivided attention and time spent with their partner. They dislike it if their partner is on their phone or otherwise distracted during dates or if they're postponing the dates often and don't offer alternatives.

2. Words of Affirmation
People who have this Love Language enjoy kind words, compliments, and verbal expressions of affection. They will, however, be very unhappy with harsh words, swearing, criticism or blaming.

3. Gifts
People who have this Love Language enjoy small gifts and the thought that was put into the gift. It's very upsetting for them if their loved one doesn't get them a birthday gift or if they're given a gift that is meaningless.

4. Acts of Service
People who have this Love Language enjoy it when someone does something for them like helping with chores at home or a project. They hate it when someone is procrastinating or promising to do things for them and doesn't come through or if their partner is lazy.

5. Physical Touch
People who have this Love Language enjoy non-sexual touch also merely being in the presence of the other person. They like hugs, being caressed, holding hands, etc. They will find it difficult if their partner is away a lot or if they rarely touch them.

* * *

A newly emerged idea presented by Molly Owns talks about Love Styles, a sort of expanded version of Love Languages. Molly Owens offers more specific examples of giving love and affection. Here are the Loves Styles proposed by her:

1. Activity
People who have this Love Style enjoy it when their partner engages in some activities with them, and they gain connection through that. They will feel unfulfilled if they pair up with someone that is a "couch potato", meaning, someone who prefers to stay home and do nothing.

2. Appreciation
People who have this Love Style enjoy compliments and the attention they get from praise; they don't like empty compliments. The

more specified and personalized the praise, the more connected they feel. This type doesn't respond very well to continuous criticism and blaming.

3. Emotional
People who have this Love Style want emotional support from their partner. They feel the most loved if they can share their emotional world and experiences and get validation and emotional exchange. It's very hard for them if they cannot connect emotionally with their partner.

4. Financial
This will include gifts but also general financial contributions to the relationship. This type will have a hard time with a stingy partner who keeps an eye on the money.

5. Intellectual
People who have this Love Style value quality time but especially intellectual exchange with partners. For them not being able to share opinions or being ridiculed for having them will be especially hurtful. If you think that's your Love Style you will be best suited for someone with similar world views or someone very open-minded.

6. Physical
People with this Love Style like non-sexual physical attention such as a hug, pat on the back or merely being in the presence of the other person. They will feel bad if their partner or a loved one is physically distant.

7. Practical
People who prefer to be given attention and love in a practical way will like it if someone helps them out with household chores, projects, or other practical issues. They dislike laziness and unfulfilled promises when it comes to tasks.

***

Finding out about Love Styles was very helpful for me because my Language is Quality Time whereas my main Love Style is Intellectual. It let me see that I prefer to spend time with people but what really shows me that there is love and connection is when I can share deep intellectual topics with others. That is why perhaps some of you will find the Love Styles slightly more insightful. All those Languages and Styles are ways in which you can be generous towards your date. If you find out early on what they prefer, you can start speaking that Language or using that Style to show your genuine interest.

Rarely a person will be proficient in all those Styles and Languages. But if from the first date you can see some signs of generosity such as attentive listening, compliments, them offering to pay, reassuring touch where it's appropriate or taking the initiative, it's a good sign. It means that your date is capable of being generous and could be willing to start speaking your Love Language or Style. Nevertheless, you need to be careful with always assuming the best. Some people can disguise toxic love bombing with generosity, so keep your wits about you and monitor for red flags even though you saw displays of generous behavior. Keep those Styles and Languages in mind and consider that you might be missing your dates' signs of generosity because they have a much different Love Language than you do.

Time for the Kiss and Time for More
Intimacy and sex are a part of a romantic relationship, which distinguishes it from friendships. The fact that we're able to touch, caress, kiss and more is an exhilarating perspective for a lot of people. Even if your libido is not very high, we all need physical touch to a certain degree. In the early stages, we're unable to tell how compatible we are when it comes to sexual drive. Emotions and hormones are running high so we can find ourselves hypersexual during that period so keep this in mind.

But let's start from the beginning. When is the best time for the first kiss? There's no one good answer to this. It can and very often is done during the first date. But not always. It really depends on your mood, your date's willingness, and the situation. If there are heaps of people around, not everyone will feel very kissy or comfortable. If you simply don't want to kiss your date, don't make yourself do things that you don't want to do; there's nothing less sexy than a demand for intimacy and obliged closeness. In your mind look for: Yes! I'm happy to do it.

Some people obviously make assumptions about the timing of the kiss. A common one is that if you don't kiss on a first date, you're not interested in each other or at least one of you isn't. Another opinion that I heard is that if a man doesn't kiss a woman on a first date, he respects her or is shy. You can see how extremely different those examples are. Just like with the problem of payment during dates, everyone comes up with their own version of the story. You need to remember that your date can have a massively different perspective than you do and, unless you ask, you can't know for sure what goes on in their mind. Even if you do ask, people can also withhold the truth for various reasons. How not to get confused?!

The healthiest option is preserving your boundaries and making the decision from your calm, curious and courageous mind. Do the Anchoring a Positive Event exercise if you're having trouble with decision making. The exercise takes a few moments, and your date doesn't even need to know about it. The same applies to the more sexual side of dating. Look for a definite Yes! that comes from wanting fun, connection, and pleasure.

If you're a people pleaser, you might tend to internalize and be on the preoccupied attachment style side. This means you might need to watch your inner Kid when you're making those decisions. Make sure that you're not agreeing because you're reluctant to lose the interest of the other person or because you want to oblige, have it over with or you want your date to develop feelings for you.

You can see that healthy reasons are more connected to self-development, pleasure, fun, and reciprocated connection with another person. Whereas unhealthy reasons are driven by fear of rejection, insecurities, people pleasing, and seeking selfish gratification. A decision made in line with your values, wants, and needs evokes good sensations and your body craves it. Whereas the unhealthy reasons are strongly related to things that aren't in your control. Perhaps you use sex as a mechanism to gain more control over the other person, the course of the relationship or maybe the situation at present. To establish if your motivation comes from a healthy Adult perspective, evoke your calmness, mindful state, and curiosity. Then see if there are any "visitors" like insecurity, fear, stress, people pleaser, inner critic, or controller.

If you know you're prone to make decisions based on opinions of your Parts rather than your calmness and curiosity, it's the time to take a step back and wait with intimacy and sex until you become more comfortable with your date. Set yourself up for a three or more dates with a no-sex rule. Even if you are not struggling with these types of issues, sex releases Oxytocin which makes us feel love and connection even if we are not objectively compatible with that sexual partner. That's why it's a good idea to get to know one another and assess if you fit together before "taking a hit" of that potent "drug".

I don't demonize sex on a first date. Nevertheless, preferring sex in long-term connected relationships and wanting to comfortably take your time to get to know the person you are dating before you engage in sexual activity is linked to a secure sexual attachment style. If there is either sexual aversion or an inability to control that urge, there can be an emotional blockage underneath those inclinations. Keep it in mind when someone offers sex to you early on.

If, however, you don't mind getting burned, you stay centered and still make good decisions regardless of sexual intimacy, by all means, choose your timing and the person. I'm aware that there's a strong pull towards people pleasing and wanting to be liked but, if the person really enjoys spending time with you, they will not mind waiting. And if they expect you to behave and restrain yourself to show that you're a good person and worthy partner and you're not into waiting for a very long time, maybe your life philosophies don't align.

If you have dramatically different outlooks on intimacy, trust, loyalty, relationships, and values perhaps you are just not the right fit for each other. Partners need to be sufficiently different so that they can challenge each other and teach things to one another, but you won't create a functional relationship with someone entirely different with a separate life path from yours. So, don't push for connection where there's none to be created. Try your luck with someone who is willing to work with you and you can see your joint path.

Also, remember that having similar libidos is very important in relationships. You obviously need trust, friendship, and good communication. Nevertheless, if you're sexually incompatible, at some point someone will get depleted because they gave too much sexually or they don't get enough. You can avoid this by making sure to choose someone who has a similar sex drive. It doesn't need to be absolutely the same in the sense that there are no rejections at all. Pick someone who is willing to put in the effort to make your sex life work.

Very often the initial stage of the relationship and dating can cloud our judgment and sex drives. The true reveal will happen within a few months when the honeymoon period wears off. So, make sure to have an honest conversation before you make everything official. Ask your partner about the importance of sex for them and perhaps even frequency and intensity that they like to have in the long term. It's not a subject for a first date, but perhaps when you do have sex and become more comfortable with each other it's good information to have about one another. Treat it as curious exploration rather than ticking boxes and interrogation.

Naturally, some people might lie, exaggerate, or downplay the truth to appear cooler or virtuous. Remember that these types of lies are short lived, and they can only hurt both you and them. Therefore, to avoid a lot of turmoil in your life, if someone asks you these types of questions, answer truthfully.

When you possess more information about the person and their outlook on sexuality you can make up your own mind much easier. As objectively as you can, establish if you can find a middle ground when it comes to sex. It's hard when hormones are still raging but that's when you need a mindful and conscious Adult state. If for instance your date is not very sexual and states that their libido is in general not very high, and you would like to have sex often, it might not be the best match even if you're very compatible in other ways. But you need to be the one weighing pros and cons.

It might seem shallow to some people, but mismatch in libido is a prevalent issue in couples that come to see me. If sex and touch is not there, you become roommates. Wouldn't it be nicer to have each other as friends? You can keep good people in your life and still pursue passion and sexual compatibility. You deserve to have both – the friendship and passion. You might currently be happy to hang around with a person who doesn't want much physical contact, but sexual hunger might not get better with time, and can sometimes breed resentment and unhappiness. So, think about the future before you get comfortable in the relationship.

By comfort I mean familiarity and feeling safe around your partner and not giving up on action. You should never be too comfortable and passive in your relationship. We obviously need to feel secure and calm while thinking about our partner, but if you're too familiar and do everything together, there's no room for novelty and excitement. The feelings of safety and excitement are the two most important components of a great sex life.

If the relationship is super new and you still feel a bit awkward, for example when being nude in front of each other this can make you nervous and impede your experience. Although when you're too familiar with each other sex can get mundane. To have a successful relationship in the future, you need to balance excitement and novelty with stability and affection for each other. Make sure to have a life outside of your relationship, your own career, hobbies and/or friends. If you don't have anything new to say or show your partner, how can you be interesting to them? If they've seen it all, if they're constantly with you, and you bring no new perspective to the table, they might as well conduct an internal dialogue and have the same outcome. And vice versa. If your partner got so comfortable that they let themselves go, has no friends, goals, career, or hobbies, and focuses solely on you, would you still be interested in him or her sexually and romantically? Having that in mind, don't let it get that far. Promote both excitement and connection in your dating life.

Sexual Difficulties and Early Dating Stages
Dating while struggling with sexual difficulties can be very tricky. Dating is perceived as the "lighthearted" period in relationships, that's why it can get awkward quickly if you are having sex with a new partner and the encounter goes south because your body doesn't want to cooperate. I consult with many people with erectile problems, ejaculation issues or vaginal pain. Having sexual problems is very common. Over 50% of men experience erectile issues at some point in life; this percentage grows when men are over 40 years old (Yetman, 2020). Premature ejaculation has around 21% of prevalence (Jannini & Lenzi, 2005) and vaginal pain during intercourse affects 10-28% of females during lifetime (Tayyeb & Gupta, 2023).

If you are suffering from any type of sexual issues or have a sexually transmitted infection (STI), it is crucial to inform your new partner about it. It would be best to hold off from sexual activity and get to know your date well before getting into the bedroom. If, however, your match wants to move on to sexual deeds quickly, you might want to get vulnerable earlier rather than later. Having a grown-up conversation about your STIs and any sexual problems that could affect both of your sexual experiences is a must. You will avoid awkward or potentially dangerous situations that you will be facing naked. It's best to talk when you are fully clothed instead of seeing the disappointment in your date's eyes when you are getting intimate.

If you are struggling with a lifelong STI like herpes, human papilloma virus or human immunodeficiency virus, your sexual partner should be aware of it and both of you should take precautions. Make sure that you use condoms, dental dams, and antiviral tablets when appropriate. It's a horrible feeling to discover this type of information after unprotected intercourse. I know it can feel confronting to be so open early on but, if you want to get close physically, the mind, practicalities and safety need to follow. If your new partner is not sympathetic and doesn't receive you well, they are probably not a great person and a partner in general. No one should make you feel like less than because of your problems.

The same goes for sexual function issues. A good partner will be supportive and help you through it instead of focusing on themselves. I know that there is strong pull towards blaming yourself when it comes to a partner's sexual issues, however, you need to see past this bias. If you partner is telling you that it's not because of you and that their body is just not listening to them at the moment, believe them. Usually, sexual difficulties are a result of stress, performance anxiety and/or unhealthy lifestyle or medical problems.

Especially when the relation between people is new, we tend to be quite stressed about sexual performance, because we fear disappointing and scaring off our match. I often hear from men that they have issues with erection or ejaculation at the beginning of a relationship and especially when they care about their new romantic mate. The less emotional involvement, the less care and stress and the better sexual function. In some ways it can be a compliment! When your new partner becomes more familiar and less stressed, their sexual function will go back to normal. That is why it's important to bring it up in the beginning so that both of you are aware of what might happen. You can also have a chat about what you can do if and when the issue arises. I suggest trying to remain in your Adult state, reassure yourself that no one is to blame and it's the time for mutual support.

Try to connect in a different way. Don't just leave the room. Talk about it, cuddle, go for a walk or do something else together. You can also drop the pedestalized intercourse, orgasm, erection, or ejaculation and focus on what sex truly is – pleasure and fun. Play with a soft penis, use your tongue and hands to pleasure one another in other ways. When you refocus on those positive aspects of sex, often the "mechanical" functions like orgasm, erection, or ejaculation are keener to join you. Remember that there is no "on" and "off" button when it comes to sexual functioning. When we are stressed and in a negative mindset when it comes to sexuality, our brain is sending messages to our genitals that read as: "It's not safe to function now, body is in danger". That's why your positive pleasure mindset needs to come first. When it comes to partner sex, you need teamwork. If one of you is freaking out, being mean or blaming themselves, your body will still feel threatened.

Going slow, keeping the connection and good communication during sex is crucial if you want to alleviate sexual problems. Check in with your partner frequently, ask them what types of touch they like, create a mental map of their body. Keep it fun and lighthearted so that there are no expectations or pressure. Before you even get to the bedroom, have a fun date where you ask each other sexual questions. Enquire about your date's sexual preferences, likes, dislikes, kinks, or insecurities. It's best if you do that at home rather than in a restaurant. Make it a fun game! If after some weeks you are still having sexual problems, contact a sex therapist like me. There are plenty of techniques and exercises that I teach my clients which help with regaining sexual confidence and function

SUMMARY

This chapter explores the importance of generosity and how it can be shown to the other person. Reciprocating affection and interest are crucial if you're considering a relationship with that person in the future. We delved into different Love Languages and Love Styles to see how you can show your date that you fancy them and start to care about them. We need to acknowledge that other people can have very different needs and want us to be generous in different ways. So, remember to ask your date about their needs and perhaps establish their Love Language or Style. Next, we talked about the "firsts," meaning the first kisses and sexual encounters. I concluded that every person needs to choose their pace based on their Adult state and what feels right for them. I also suggested not to make that decision from the place of lack, insecurity, people pleasing or opinions of others. Opinions can be taken into consideration, nevertheless they don't need to be followed if the advice doesn't feel right for you. Lastly, we talked about sexual difficulties and STIs when it comes to intimacy in early dating.

Chapter 16:
Be Aware of Ghosting Realities

Remember that often people might not mean things they say during the initial encounter for various reasons. Perhaps they want to be polite or they're in a rush. They might also change their mind between now and later in the week or even in a day. Rejection can come at any point. Because of that, the word "ghosting" was invented. Ghosting is ignoring your date, not responding to their texts, and cutting any type of contact without an explanation. Whether we like it or not, it's both common to do this to someone else and to have it done to you. It's good to be aware of this phenomenon as well as to develop the right mindset to avoid emotional hardship if you're faced with this type of rejection. I'll also provide you with an exercise that will help you to achieve a mindset of acceptance, and forgiveness that lets you move on from emotional hardship. In this chapter we explore both sides of ghosting: the reasons why some do it and the feelings of those who have it done to them. Lastly, I discuss how to approach being ghosted and whether it can ever be acceptable to reject others this way. This chapter will focus on online dating, but in reality, ghosting happens in any type of dating experience.

Let's explore some reasons for ghosting from the perspective of the people performing the ghosting and the rejected individuals. Ghosting as a word emerged relatively recently with the development of online dating. But similar situations can be found in the literature created before the internet (Timmermans et al., 2020). Nevertheless, we need to acknowledge that it made it so much easier to ignore and never meet the rejected person again. The majority are no longer living in small villages where everyone knows each other. There's no negative social bearing and consequences that are waiting for us if we chose to ghost someone. Online you can meet perfect strangers and the pool of options is massive, but this gives more room for lack of accountability. Lack of physical contact seems to be a big catalyst for ghosting and forgetting that others are human beings, not merely images. To stop this bias, think how you would feel if another person considered you not entirely human and insignificant.

A study conducted by Timmermans, Hermans and Opree (2020) focused on online dating. They found that mobile daters who were ghosted in the past mostly (59%) externalised by assuming that the ghoster was talking to someone else, was not interested or too busy to respond or they marked this person as rude, lazy, or childish. Fewer people, but still a significant number, (37%) internalized the rejection by self-deprecating and attacking their own appearance and personality or brought up a possibility of lack of response because of their rejection of the ghoster's sexual advances. The remaining 17% talked about how easy it is for people to ghost online and that pool of options can contribute to the phenomenon. This shows how common internalization and externalization still are in the dating world.

The truth is you most likely will never find out exactly why someone ghosted you. Targeting yourself or another person builds up resentment towards not only you and them, but also towards the whole concept of dating. If you build up enough anger and sadness, you will quickly fall into dating burnout. Mindful acceptance is what you want your perspective to be. To practice it perform the exercise below.

* * *

EXERCISE: Mindful Acceptance Exercise
Mindful Acceptance is when you choose to accept things, even though there are some Parts of you that don't want to do it. When you're faced

with being ghosted or other type of rejection, try to acknowledge if you're externalizing or internalizing. Recognize those practices are dysfunctional and choose another path purposefully. Go back to what you know rather than what you assume. Try to be as logical during your thought processes as possible.

Facts:
- It's easier to ghost on dating apps.
- Ghosting is a common occurrence.
- I don't know what the person's reasons are for ghosting me and it's possible to move on without a conversation about it. There are different steps of closure so create your own healing plan. Or use the 10 Step Post Rejection Recuperation Plan available in Part 1 Chapter 3.
- There's a possibility that ghosting had nothing to do with you.
- It's possible that, despite ghosting me, this person is a decent human being.

Repeating sentences like this will bring you closer to a balanced state. Mindful Acceptance requires you to be non-judgmental, intentional in your thoughts and focused on the current moment.

* * *

Instead of focusing your precious energy on attacking yourself or others, direct it towards the ability to heal and calming your inner Kid. Your internal Parts were most likely very riled up because ghosting is a message that someone doesn't want to spend their time in our company anymore. We also don't handle uncertainty very well. Not knowing why, we were ghosted can be unsettling in so many ways. People can experience various symptoms such as anxiety, depression, anger, lowered self-esteem, or some will even start altering their life choices . Emotional dysregulation comes from events like that but can be managed by Mindful Acceptance.

Now that we know the perspective of people who have been ghosted. Let's get to know the other side of the story. Timmermans, Hermans and Opree (2020) also found that the younger people are, the more likely they're to ghost. In addition, the less time they spend on dating apps, the more likely they were to ignore their match.

Ghosters seem to also be mainly externalizers, 67% blamed it on the person that they ghosted. There were five different categories that externalizing ghosters fit into. The first category was the largest, and the rest grow progressively smaller. The first one mentioned the ghostee's personality characterizing them as boring, quickly falling in love or a person with problems such as fear of committing. The second category focused on undesired actions and behaviors performed by the person who they've ghosted. This category described things like rudeness, racism, sending unwanted messages with sexual content, lying, or refusing to accept reasons for rejecting them. Therefore, some of these folks didn't see any other option but to ghost. In the third subgroup category people reported finding out that they did not share their date's intentions. The next category didn't enjoy the date itself and the last one focused on the ghostee as unattractive.

The second subgroup of ghosters blamed the ghosting on themselves. This subgroup was somewhat smaller than the one described above. Some of the respondents wanted to protect themselves from backlash, stalking and confrontation in general. Another lot didn't feel ready to date or was afraid to not meet the other person's expectations. Others feared manipulation from the ghosted person. The second big theme that emerged in the internalizing subgroup was subsequent interest in another person and forgetting about the ghosted person. Some individuals also stated that they were too busy to respond.

The third subgroup of ghosters mainly focused on the app features. They blamed the ease of online ghosting, the massive option pool and lack of social connection with the match. People from this subgroup also said that they've deleted the whole app and lost all the conversations.

The fourth subgroup was slightly smaller than the third one. People in this subgroup lacked any feeling of obligation to respond to the ghosted person.

The fifth subgroup was similar in size to the fourth group. Those people didn't want to hurt the feelings of their match and it seemed easier to stop responding to avoid humiliating them.

The main difference between the two largest groups of ghosters and ghostees is that the first one did not experience the surprise and uncertainty of the rejection; their world view and introspection was not submitted to turmoil. They used their opinions to determine whether they would like to see this person again. And they have a right to choose freely, perhaps sometimes they truly didn't have another choice or didn't want to lie about the reasons or hurt someone even more deeply with the truth. Some individuals did report preference for ghosting instead of hearing uncomfortable truths about other people's perception of them. Other research has found that people who are rejecting also can experience a lot of discomfort and difficult emotions especially when they fear backlash (Bohns & DeVincent, 2018).

People generally didn't mind ghosting if it was performed before face-to-face contact and within two days (Timmermans et al., 2020). These criteria meant that there was no commitment and no time for emotions to be formed. This definition of a "ghosting window period" can obviously vary from person to person, but there seems to be some level of acceptance towards it in society.

Thinking of others is important especially if we want to address the problems in contemporary dating, and ghosting is often an inconsiderate and unkind thing to do to the other person. Most people are reluctant to be the start of the change because "no one else is doing it!" (Sounds to me like your inner Kid is back). Nevertheless, if you look at things more holistically, keeping balance and honesty towards yourself and others is important for personal growth, which in turn helps you to date in a healthy way and find the most fulfilling relationships.

It takes courage and wholeheartedness to care at least in some degree for people who you don't know very well. Remember that they're still human beings. Remember that you're creating this culture for your current or future kids or for future generations. If you don't care about anything like this at all, it means that you're not a fully functional Adult. If the only thing that you care about is yourself, you're on grandiosity territory, which as we know already leads you away from connection and fulfillment. It also means that you're leading your life through your grandiose and selfish Part. Look up from your, let's be honest, mostly comfortable Western society life and get curious about something greater. Of course, we suffer in some ways, but if you have the capacity to think about dating and looking for love, you have the capacity to better yourself for the greater good of others and our culture.

Start with honesty, compassion and understanding. Nevertheless, it's also important to realize that honesty doesn't have to be cruel. Perhaps you want to leave out some hurtful details when you break the news to the person you're rejecting or add something caring. Sometimes there is no way to put things in a kinder way, which is why people often lie out of care for others, but also to spare themselves the feeling of guilt for hurting another person. Even though a lie is the opposite of honesty, it can correspond with consideration for others. You need to be the judge of what's the best solution for both you and the person you're rejecting. Your only points of reference are your own experience and perhaps some advice from friends. There's no way for us to know what type of rejection the other person would prefer.

A common view is that we don't owe our short-term dating partners explanations because the short amount of contact could not elicit strong emotions. Nonetheless, we have no knowledge about the internal world of anyone other than ourselves, unless we ask, which we rarely do especially, at the beginning of the relation.

The right thing to do can be confusing and take many forms. It all depends on your situation. Honest rejection can also make people realize some things about themselves that can be changed and improved. For example, if a fifth woman rejects you because you sent her an uncalled-for dick pic, perhaps you can acknowledge that not everyone enjoys those, especially not at the beginning of a friendship. Or if you get rejected again because you posted decade-old photos on your dating profile, maybe it's time to be more honest.

Rejections can be useful if we're able to handle them gracefully and allow the other person to make their choice. If you're not beating yourself up or blaming others, you can devote this space to contemplating a change for the better. Acknowledge what can be changed and focus on it. Perhaps this perspective can also encourage people to stop ghosting and let the other person know what went wrong and where they could improve next time.

If you're ghosting because of a factor that can't be changed, a simple "I'm sorry, but I'm just not feeling it," is sufficient. I've met plenty of handsome men who were good on paper, but there was no connection. Either conversation was not flowing, jokes were misunderstood, or our values were too different. It's no one's fault that chemistry and emotional connection didn't appear. In many cases we really don't have to point a finger at anyone but acknowledge that we had some unfulfilled hope. Just because the other person isn't a suitable partner for us, doesn't mean that we should insult them or blame them for ghosting them.

I hope that I convinced you to avoid ghosting, at least in most situations. We can create a better dating environment for everyone and practice kind honesty. If everyone thinks about how they would like to be treated and then apply it to others, we could solve a lot of issues. I urge you to perform kind acts not only towards others, but also toward yourself to promote good mental health. This will also make you an awesome and connected partner.

If there is a Part of you that was perhaps wronged in the past and wishes to hurt others because of it, and that's why you are practicing cruelty in dating, it needs to be addressed. A true hero doesn't want to hurt others because of their difficult past but wants to protect them from the same pain. A villain will explain their bad behavior with what they went through. We often don't realize that we are just taking dysfunctional revenge on humanity, believe me I know how oblivious one can get, I'm a reformed villain myself. It's never too late to look in the mirror and see what needs to change, but we are often too afraid and avert the gaze.

Perhaps this study (Timmermans et al., 2020) and my thoughts on ghosting will help you face rejections with Mindful Acceptance instead of experiencing a pointless guessing game and maybe, if the situation allows for it, some notorious ghosters will be more honest in the future.

SUMMARY

The chapter defined ghosting and stressed that it's not a kind thing to do to others. I acknowledged, however, that in some cases people lacked another option. I've also presented you with an exercise that will bring you to a state of Mindful Acceptance when faced with being ghosted. This chapter focused on ghosting in context of on online dating. We have also explored different thought processes that people have when ghosting which range from blaming others, themselves, or the online apps for the ease of ghosting. We also explored the emotional world of people who have been ghosted. Lastly, we discussed the toxicity of ghosting for society in general and the effects of showing a lack of consideration for others. Hopefully I convinced you to treat others with respect and kindness whenever possible.

Chapter 17:
Handling Tricky Dating Situations

This chapter is devoted to difficult situations that you might face while dating. We discuss how to gently reject people who we don't want to form a romantic relationship with. We talk about handling a person who has resurfaced on our dating radar after a long absence. Next, we delve into how to reengage in dating after a breakup. Lastly, I'll discuss some courses of action if your date or partner has a lot of opposite sex friends, and it's bothering you. I hope those thought and tips will help you to use the right mindset if you find yourself in these situations.

Letting People Down Gracefully
Now that you know how to read the signals and behave, you'll also need to be able to handle situations when you want to reject someone else. With this book I want to promote a moral and safe dating culture for everyone. It's not always nice and fuzzy when you're using all your courage to put yourself out there. It's just good practice to leave the scene without a bitter aftertaste, kind of like paying it forward. You don't like nasty rejections; other people also have similar preferences. Let's hope that future generations will be much nicer to each other, and we can start this change now by acting better.

It's allowed to dislike someone. Whether we like it or not, it will happen often. The problem begins when we want to let the other person know about our lack of fondness for them. It already sounds hurtful, doesn't it?

There are couple of ways to approach rejecting people. We already discussed ghosting. I do not recommend this type of rejection. Nevertheless, if you can't avoid it because the other person will not take no for an answer or you're in some ways afraid of them, then it's a last resort.

The next way to reject others is through direct conversation or at least stating some reasons for ceasing the association. It can happen through a message, phone call or an in-person meeting. The more effort we put into the ending of an acquaintance, the more polite it is considered by society. But we're also socially required to put in more effort if the relationship is longer and more meaningful. So, if you have been seeing someone for a few months and there was more commitment, it's nice to do it in person. However, if you just started dating and after a couple of meetings you want to end the relationship, people often don't mind a phone call or a text message, though the preference is subjective.

Try a simple "I had a nice time with you, but I don't think I want to pursue things further. I'm sorry." Or some sort of variation of it should be informative enough. Especially if it wasn't your date's fault, and he or she was well behaved and polite, there's no reason to be confrontational or to ghost. If your date's poor behavior is the reason, you're severing contact, it's good practice to include constructive feedback by focusing on specific behaviors and your own feelings, rather than on blaming or shaming them. You don't want to aggravate anyone but simply give some feedback about what they could improve next time. People are much more prone to take things into consideration if they're said kindly and firmly. You might make this person think about their behavior and perhaps even improve their dating experience later on.

It's obviously not a rule and you won't change everyone, but people get away without reprimands all too often and start to believe that they can behave poorly. So, I don't want you to go around screaming at each other, but a couple of calm remarks can be a way to go. If your date starts to present signs of poor communication, retaliates, or ignores your comment, you can always politely leave the conversation. If, however, you feel intimidated by your date, I wouldn't recommend traumatizing yourself further. In this case, stick to a simple rejection.

I don't believe there's much point to say all the uncomfortable and unchangeable truths. Perhaps you don't like the way that person looks, and it can't be changed. If they present some views or traits that are not offensive but you two are misaligned in some very important way, you can comfortably say that you would not be a great couple in general. You will need to choose if a certain reason is worth mentioning.

There are also things that aren't very invasive, and we just have different life paths. For example, some people don't want to have children at all and for another person it's an absolute must. Our biological clocks are ticking, for women even faster, so you might not want to start a long-term relationship with people who clearly have different life path.

Nonetheless, if a person requires an explanation and is very persistent about it, then it will be up to you to decide how much you want to tell them. Truth can be hurtful, but we can try to be as polite as possible. Or you can choose to state part of the reason and leave out the most hurtful and non-changeable aspects. Either way, it's a moral call. My suggestions are opinions, and you must decide if you agree with them.

Some people would want to leave very quickly after meeting their date. A polite thing to do is usually to give it a go for an hour or so. Nevertheless, if your date for instance catfished you or is simply unbearable because of poor behavior, lack of tact or inappropriate views, you might find yourself in a situation where you would like to escape through a bathroom window. It can call for drastic measures, an escape plan, or an excuse. If you feel intimidated by your date and you don't know what to do, it's good to have the plan ready.

You might want to have a trusted friend on standby to call you and pretend that there was an emergency. You can even just discreetly leave the premises. Or ask the bar or restaurant staff for help when it comes to ordering a taxi. You can also state that something important has come up and you need to leave immediately after checking your phone. If the person starts to question you, you don't have to answer all their enquiries.

Politely repeat that you simply must go and leave the scene. Your priority is your safety and comfort during those situations. Even if your date didn't plan on making you feel that way or escalating things, there's no harm in precaution. Making sure that you feel safe takes precedence over your date's feelings in that case.

Nevertheless, if you're not feeling uneasy but simply bored and want to leave, then you have the capacity to bring your date's feelings into the equation. We all had those dates where we are eager for an exit. Remember that dates don't need to be long so perhaps it won't be too painful to wait thirty minutes and politely reject them.

The second option is more confrontational, but it saves you time and hardship during the meeting. It can put you in a vulnerable position where you might be required to answer some questions or face an outburst, but as previously discussed, vulnerability is a sign of courage.

If you put yourself out there like this, you will have much more experience with difficult conversations and situations that can turn you into a better and more responsible and capable person. So, the less you run away now, facing your issues and new situations head on, the better partner and possibly parent you can be. Treat it as a character-building exercise. If you can gracefully and politely reject someone, you might also be able to understand people who reject you and take it more gracefully in the future.

There's no one recipe for a kind and graceful rejection. Many factors come into this decision such as your safety, the type of date you are with and your location. So, make sure to account for every element and figure out the kindest and quickest way to remove yourself from the situation. If you chose to go on a hike and there's no other way back, you might want to wait it out. It will be rather uncomfortable for the both of you if you reject your date midway. Use your common sense and moral compass and that should suffice.

Handling a Blast from the Past
Deciding whether to let someone back into your life will depend on several factors. Ask yourself a few questions before you make a final decision:

1) Is it worth it to pursue this again?
2) Am I making a decision from my emotions instead of my Adult mode?
3) Did we or could we have a true connection in the future?
4) What were the external circumstances at the time of losing contact?

First, listen to your Adult self. You don't have to let this person back into your life but perhaps you crave an explanation or closure? You can ask for that and make your decision later. Having a person come back after weeks or months of not talking to you or not dating is a very common occurrence. A lot of the times this person might resurface because they seek attention and validation. Some might have disappeared because of some external circumstances or the fact that they were unprepared for more than they already gave last time.

If you have no feelings towards that person and you don't feel like you want answers or to explore the possibilities, by all means, keep them out of your life. But if you choose to reengage, make sure to address the absenteeism. If you pretend nothing happened, you give them permission to disappear again in the future. Make sure that they explain themselves and validate your feelings towards their actions. If they make amends and you consider their explanation to be sufficient and appropriate, you will be clearing the air. I'm a firm believer in "right person at the wrong time". Perhaps one or both of you were not ready for the next step or there were some external circumstances that kept you apart. It's fine to give the right person a second chance. But not a third and fourth. If you find that you're forgiving and letting them in repeatedly, they're most likely not the right person. You also need to establish together how you will not let it happen again and what went wrong.

Dating After a Breakup

Are you just getting back in the game after having your heart broken? Let's break it down for you so you'll be able to navigate those situations better. Breaking a bond with someone for whatever reason is very painful, not only emotionally but our body can feel it too. You are basically starting a rehab so expect withdrawal symptoms. That's why so many people will want to get back with their ex-partners even though they're aware that it's the worst idea. The pain can be so deep that we lose our sense of self, and we need to find our way back. You just lost a big factor from your life, your hopes, and dreams along with it. Your brain chemistry is all over the place because our partners were giving us consistent hits of dopamine that are now taken away.

It's normal to be angry and resentful, but at the same time long for and miss that person. I see this duality in my clients, friends, and myself. I find that the quicker you accept and make space for those emotions, the more efficiently you can heal. People who use unhealthy coping mechanisms like repressing feelings or using addictions to mask how much they're hurting will have a prolonged healing journey. If you don't face your pain, it will wait for you until you will be able to look it in the eye. Until then, this festering pain will spill over into your life through anger issues or the inability to connect to others or to enjoy your life.

I also find that the more people try to expedite the healing process, the more time it takes them to heal. So don't try to time your inner journey. There isn't only one closure during a breakup. I felt milestone closures many times when I was healing after a relationship. So, acknowledge and cherish each of the feelings of release and closure but don't presume it's your last. Perhaps you wrote them a last message as their partner, you picked up your things, you went on a first date after a breakup or kissed a new person. All those things will be your closures. Each might feel like you're getting there, and each will be less painful if you're healing in a healthy way.

Allow yourself to grieve in your own unique way. Listen to your body and make sure that it's a way that will not hurt you or others in any other manner. Grief has stages and you might find yourself between them sometimes. It's easy to lock yourself in the cycle of longing and anger when losing someone. A way out for me was to forgive myself for what I did wrong, make amends, and forgive my exes as well. Creating a good relationship with yourself will be crucial for you because we often break our boundaries during breakups.

There are different models of stages of grief but most mention (Kübler-Ross & Kessler, 2014):
1) Shock/Denial
2) Bargaining and Longing
3) Anger
4) Depression
5) Acceptance & Adjustment

Don't be alarmed if you thought that you have fully moved on when this person pops into your head. It's okay if it happens! They were a big part of your life; you cannot erase them. Problems begin when you try to throw them out of your mind. This way you only solidify their effect on you. The following exercise is often used by therapists to make you realize how intrusive thoughts work in your mind. The theory behind it's called "ironic process theory" was described first by Daniel Wegner (Wegner, 1994). It talks about how suppressing thoughts can make them even more intrusive. We can evoke and promote the frequency of feeling of all our emotions to a certain degree, positive and difficult ones. Nevertheless, I find that a lot of my clients tend to hyperfocus on the negative sensations and therefore promote them in their mind. We perceive difficult feelings as a threat and try to "fix" them. It's important to understand that emotions can't be "fixed"; they just "are". It's best to focus on understanding your emotions, validating them, fulfilling their needs, and letting them just "be". To help you understand this concept please perform the exercise below.

* * *

EXERCISE: Pink Elephant Exercise (Rose, 2022)
Try very hard not to think about a pink elephant.
 What happened?
 A pink elephant popped into your head, didn't it?
This is what happens when you don't want to think or feel something. That's why anxiety is so tricky to control. The more you fear it and

the more you don't want it, the more it comes in. So, practice Mindful Acceptance. If your ex comes to your mind, acknowledge it, accept it, and move on with your day. Not a big deal!

* * *

To handle your emotional world after a breakup, use the Post Rejection Recuperation Plan. It was a great help to me in making plenty of plans with my friends, meeting new people, keeping healthy and being creative at work. But at what stage should you reengage in the dating world?

I think everyone needs to answer this question for themselves through listening to their inner Adult. Make sure that your judgement is not clouded by loneliness, anger, resentment, or fear. If you do choose to go back to dating straight away, remember to do it safely and mindfully. Listen to what your body wants. You might be keen to meet new people but ask yourself if you're ready for a physical connection. Most likely you won't be ready to jump into a new relationship straight away, even though a Part of you disagrees. Maybe jumping straight back into dating multiple people is just a distraction from the pain?

If you were with someone for a long time you might feel depleted and invested in that person. So don't try to invest even more in someone new just because you feel lonely; you most likely don't have enough energy to give at that stage. Some people, however, might be moving on already while still in the relationship, so perhaps you're moving on quicker because you started the detachment process a while ago. Let yourself grieve and acknowledge your own level of processing.

It's fine just to enjoy people's company without leading the other person on for attention or sexual gratification so be honest about your intentions with others when you realize them. Give yourself some time in between dates to listen to your emotions and unmet needs. Remember that you will be floating around different moods, and your Parts can visit you randomly. One day you might feel awesome, accepting and "zen" but another week can bring anger and resentment once again. Accept this fluidity and think of bad days as periods of time and not a sign of regression. Eventually, there will be more good days than bad days when it comes to relationship ruminations and someone else will be able to take over this romantic space in your mind.

When Your Date Has a Lot of Opposite Sex Friends
I did not put this in the red flags list because this doesn't need to be a bad sign. The tricky part is to recognize if your date is in fact friends with these women or men or if there are some other sexual arrangements. I think friendships between women and men are very possible and can enrich lives of both parties. Just because one or both of you considers each other attractive, it doesn't mean that you will be a good couple.

If both of you acknowledge that you'll never work as romantic or sexual partners, you can focus on building your friendship and enjoying the benefits of it. I find that there are plenty of reasons to have opposite sex friends. As a woman, I can get a male's perspective on life and dating very easily, which broadens my horizons when it comes to understanding not only my dates and also my male clients. I often introduce my single girlfriends to my boy-mates, and they do the same for me.

To have this type of friendship successfully, one needs a certain level of maturity to put aside some thoughts and desires which will never be fulfilled, and to focus on what's possible. Nevertheless, there are many people who portray themselves as capable of those friendships when in fact they are not and are only using this illusion to explain their various casual sex arrangements.

The latter kind of people will reveal themselves when it comes to the test of consistency in their affection and putting you first as a romantic partner. If they seem to prioritize their "friendships" over you the majority of the time and neglect to validate your feelings of insecurity, they might be showing you a red flag. If you bring up your insecurity calmly and kindly, a good partner should be able to talk about it and help you not to feel that way by reassuring you and coming up with some future solutions.

SUMMARY

This chapter explored a few different tricky dating situations that may happen to anyone. We discussed how to gracefully reject others to minimize damage, while not bending our boundaries. I also brought up a scenario where an old flame resurfaces in your dating life, and you want to let them back in, but you struggle to decide if and how you should do it. Subsequently, we discussed the realities and a healthy mindset when it comes to dating after a recent breakup. Lastly, I talked about a scenario where your date has a lot of opposite sex friendships which bothers you. We explored different courses of actions, perspectives, and emotional regulation. Hopefully those pointers will help you navigate those tricky situations.

Chapter 18:
Can You Bleach a Red Flag?

This chapter explores red flags to watch out for in a partner but also within yourself. The point of this book is to make you the best dater possible and that entails that you hold yourself to the same standards as you hold your prospective dates and partners. I'll discuss how to recognize each red flag, if there's any hope for changing it, and identify the remedies. Often, we might see some bad signs, but it doesn't mean that people can't change and learn how they should treat you. You need to be the teacher; only that way you can check if you can change the color of that red flag to yellow and for it to eventually disappear. I'll bring up the most common examples of red flags in people. But don't think that this list ends there.

I realize how hard it can be, especially in the beginning, to read green and red flags properly. It can sometimes take a few dates to realize that this funny but edgy joke that your date told was in fact a way of checking your reaction so they can reveal their dark side. Similarly, if they said something out of turn, it might reflect nothing more than nervousness. How to check if it was a harmless slip or a red flag?

Look for consistency and patterns. If they performed similar questionable behavior more than twice, you can start considering behavioral patterns. Some actions don't require you to wait for the second and third time. If the person is outright rude and offensive, it's time to run straight after the first incident. However, if you're unsure and want to give this person a second chance, then make sure to keep that incident in mind so that you can compare it to other ones in the future.

I had many requests from my clients for this list. I'll do my best to include as many examples as possible, but it doesn't mean I've covered them all. You will need to make the executive decision when it comes to your dates; I can only give you some clues and examples. True skill and recognition come with practice but also with self-development. If you did your inner work, you know how to implement boundaries and what you want in a partner. That's why the first part of this book is so vital.

This list should help you to weed out the narcissistic types and people who are very high on the preoccupied or avoidant attachment style spectrum. Those people definitely need more inner work and self-reflection and aren't ready to form good stable relationships. Highly narcissistic people will only take and bring in toxicity. Highly avoidant people won't be able to connect. And the Preoccupied types will make excessive demands.

Again, if you make your boundaries clear and strong from the beginning you should be able to quickly determine who is who. People high in narcissism will run away from you exceptionally fast. They fear self-aware people because someone who is self-assured and self-actualized has a strong sense of reality, whereas people with narcissistic traits or a disorder have a skewed perception of the world where they are the gods. If you make them realize quickly that they cannot implant their distorted views in you, they'll move on to the next person. The Preoccupied can cling on to you, but your boundaries won't allow you to maintain contact with them. And Avoidants will simply avoid their way out because with your great boundaries you will not chase them.

It all comes down to boundaries! If you have those in place you can be connected and safe at the same. It may be difficult to implement those especially with people who already know you. You have been displaying certain behaviors for most of your life, so people can be confused when you change and even push back. Changing your behavior to display healthy patterns will very likely also weed out bad friends and family members and dysfunctional patterns in those relationships. You need to be prepared for a change not only in your actions but also in how your environment adjusts to the "new you".

Some people might become more distant or absent. Some, on the other hand, might deepen their emotional relationship with you. That's the beauty of positive change. You can deepen the connections that serve you well and weaken the contact with people who are draining and unhealthy for you. To truly transform your life in that way, you need to give it time and consistency. You can't do this halfway. If people see that your pattern is patchy, they might exploit it or ignore it. The trick is to not let them ignore your boundaries. If you're still struggling with wobbly boundaries, you might need to put in place some consequences for people who do not respect them and stick to them. You can allow the people who respect your wishes back into your world while the ones that choose to ignore them will need to stay behind the line. By being the authentic "you" with new boundaries, you will find others with similar values much easier. This also applies in dating.

The great thing about dating is that it's fresh and new. You're just getting to know this person. They have no idea about your past patterns and behaviors, so they're prepared to accept the new knowledge and adjust accordingly or leave the scene. You can be the "new you" without the hovering past.

So, remember that you need to be upfront about your feelings and needs and the behavioral standards that you require from those around you. We should constantly negotiate with our dates and partners. Working on a red flag may also mean going to therapy together. I know that in dating you don't want to be talking about it, but if you encounter someone with a red flag and you simply cannot (or as I teach people to say "chose not to") let go of them, at least press for a change, and bring up therapy if you want to exhaust all your options.

Now that you know how to handle yourself, you must learn how to recognize warning signs in others. The crucial thing is to recognize early signs of abuse. If you don't pay attention to abusive behaviors, you might end up in a very dangerous situation physically, emotionally, financially, and socially. Here are different types of abuse, make a mental note of them and run from anyone that exhibits such behaviors.

Abuse Red Flags

Psychological Abuse
- Gaslighting – manipulating you into doubting your own sanity.
- Playing mind games with you.
- Twisting things around so nothing is their fault and you're the cause of their outburst.
- Accusing you of doing things you haven't done.
- Constantly lying.
- Threatening to harm you, your kids, or pets.

Emotional Abuse
- Insulting you.
- Constantly putting you down.
- Intimidating you.
- Embarrassing you in front of other people.
- Talking down to you.
- Not listening or respecting your feelings.
- Blaming you for every issue and not seeing their own faults.

Verbal Abuse
- Yelling, shouting, and swearing at you.
- Continuously looking for reasons to argue.
- Interrupting you.
- Talking over you.
- Using loud, threatening language & tones to cause fear.
- Calling you names.
- Mocking you.

Financial Abuse
- Shaming you for how you spend money.
- Not wanting you to further your education or to work.
- Not wanting you to own a car.

Religious Abuse
- Denying and/or misusing religious beliefs.
- Interpreting beliefs in a way which forces you into subordinate roles.
- Misusing religion or spiritual traditions to justify physical violence or other abuse.
- Forbidding you to practice your own religion.
- Insulting your religion and or spiritual beliefs.
- Using your religion to shame you.

Social Abuse
- Forbidding you to have friends or meet other people.
- Forbidding you to network.
- Forbidding you from attending events.

Unfortunately, these types of abuse are often overlooked not only by the courts but also by the victims who may think it's a normal relationship pattern. A lot of victims come from abusive families and abuse is familiar and normal to them. When the perpetrator sees that they can get away with this type of behavior, more extreme types of abuse may occur as well such as:

Physical Abuse
- Kicking, punching, biting, slapping, grabbing, chocking, or pulling your hair.
- Standing over you or getting "In your face".
- Blocking a door and not allowing you to leave.
- Grabbing you and threatening to harm you.
- Threatening you with a weapon.
- Burning or threatening to burn you.

Sexual Abuse
- Committing rape, attempted rape, or sexual assault,
- Inappropriate touching anywhere on the body.

- Performing non-consensual masturbation of either or both persons.
- Performing any sexual activity that the person lacks the capacity to consent to.
- Engaging in inappropriate looking, sexual teasing, or sexual harassment.
- Forcing use of pornography or witnessing of sexual acts.
- Engaging in indecent exposure.

Narcissism Red Flags
In this chapter we discuss subtle narcissistic red flags that might not be as visible as the extreme forms of violence and abuse described above. Bear in mind that narcissists could potentially exhibit the above abusive behaviors as well. This is not only a list of behaviors that people with Narcissistic Disorder exhibit. We are still talking about people high in narcissistic traits in general. We explore each of those red flags in depth and discuss ways to address them.

☞ They belittle you jokingly.
The beginning of dating should be especially polite, so if someone is already testing you, that's a bad sign. Someone that truly likes you and is capable of a secure and functional relationship will not belittle you, even as a joke. Perhaps down the track you might develop inside jokes that will involve some play with picking on each other, but that has a different emotional bearing when it's done in a secure long-term relationship. You can point it out to your date; perhaps their humor is edgy. But when you bring this to their attention, they need to acknowledge it and validate your experience and negotiate the edginess to not to make you feel uncomfortable. If, however, they point a finger at you and say that you exaggerate, it's a sign this flag will remain red, so run!

☞ They make you doubt your sense of reality AKA Gaslighting.
They don't take your perspective into consideration and push towards complete control over what's real and what's not. As a counsellor I see

couples with massive differences in perspectives. A considerate partner skilled in communication will be able to take your view into consideration even though they disagree with you. If you can see that your date is not doing it on purpose, you can try teaching them about seeing perspectives and internalization. But if they're hellbent on pushing their view on to you and ridicule your ideas and views, you're dealing with gaslighting, so I recommend you leave.

☞ Trying to make you jealous.
Narcissists will play mind tricks on you and jealousy usually elicits a big response in people. The more response they see, the more perceived control they feel over you. They also might gaslight you in the process by making you feel bad for feeling jealous. It means that the red flag is unwavering. You can confront them about it and talk about your feelings, some people don't try to make us jealous on purpose. So, make sure that you are talking about your emotional experience and their behavior. If they validate and acknowledge your feelings and negotiate a change in behavior, it could mean the red flag can be bleached.

☞ Gossiping and ill wishing.
Often narcissistic types will be trying to control their environment by subtly talking about others in negative ways. If during early stages, they engage in social slurring in front of you, you can't be sure if they won't do the same to you. When you're in a long-term relationship, and you know each other better, there might be times when you just really want to vent about this jerk at work. But if you can see a frequent pattern that includes gossiping and ill wishing people from many different areas of life, it might be a red flag even in your long-term relationship. You can enquire about a change in behavior, but if someone engages in frequent criticism of self and others, it means that there could be deeper issues from childhood that would need to be resolved for the change to be permanent.

☞ Comparing you to their ex-partner.
Even though some positive comparisons can be used as a compliment, it's good to refrain from comparisons like this in general during the beginning phase of the relationship. People who negatively compare you, even in subtle ways, can be showing you a red flag. You can negotiate a change in behavior but if your date makes you feel bad for bringing it up or avoids the topic, run!

☞ Talking badly about their exes.
It's a bad sign if your date is badmouthing their ex-partners, especially if they do it early on. The fact is some people just had it very tough in relationships and maybe they have tendency to choose narcissists and cruel people. Sometimes, no matter how good the partner was, a person with narcissistic traits might demonize everything about their exes. Nothing is ever their fault, so clearly it had to be the ex. If that's the case, it's a clear narcissistic red flag. If, however, you see that your date is good person with nasty exes, they might not be narcissistic. Nevertheless, it's good to think about why this person chose these types of partners in the first place. Perhaps there's some other red flag or unresolved trauma. Dig deeper to find out more before you decide to start a relationship with that person.

☞ Being unkind to other people, especially in front of you.
If you heard a gossip about your date being unkind, there can be a second layer to it. But if you witness your date being outright rude, inconsiderate or in general behaving poorly without an appropriate reason like being provoked, it can be a red flag. During early dating, we want to show ourselves from the best angle. If your date doesn't do it, they might already be showing you their true self. You can try negotiating, but those types of issues, just like being overly critical, can run very deep so this person would most likely need to sort out their issues in therapy.

☞ Love bombing.
Generosity is good and we all need a generous partner, but, if it seems like the person wants to buy your affection and goes over the top, it might be

a red flag in disguise. Often people with a fearful attachment style will also resort to love bombing to push and pull in the relationship. Being hot and cold in the relationship can create a "trauma bond" with the narcissist who is trying to lure you emotionally closer to them. If you catch yourself saying: "It's so good when it's good. But when it's bad it's very bad" you are very likely in a toxic relationship. Highs and lows can give your brain the idea that no one has ever been so in love like the two of you. This, however, is an illusion created by massive discrepancies in the good and bad times. Truly healthy and stable relationships will be exactly this – stable. You might catch yourself saying "we are good and solid" even if there was an argument earlier. Bad times in stable relationships are usually connected to external factors or are not that significant because both of you can communicate functionally and care deeply about one another. If it feels like a swing of highs and lows, it isn't good for you. Overpromising, talking about serious plans like engagement, having kids and moving in together when there was not enough time to form connection are also inappropriate.

☞ Making you feel ungrateful and glorifying deeds performed for you.
If you say, please and thank you like any other polite human being, you don't have to bend over backwards to show people your gratitude for the next six months for booking a table. It's a mind game that narcissists play to make you feel like you're indebted to them. They might bring up the smallest good deeds and sometimes even obvious things that should be done by any mediocre partner. They will make those tiny favors look like God's greatest gift, so you need to look past the words and see the reality. They might also make you feel ungrateful if you don't entertain that unrealistic power trip.

☞ Disrespecting your boundaries.
Everyone to a certain degree will be looking for your limits because they also need to be sure how to act around you. Problems begin when you state your boundary, and it gets ignored. There's obviously a learning

and adjustment period, but if you can see that you've been placing your boundary, and your date has pushed it more than couple of times, you might be dealing with their dysfunctional pattern of behavior, which is a red flag.

☞ Initial interest and self-centered behaviors.
At the beginning, narcissists might put on a mask and will be seemingly very much interested in what you have to say to get to know how they can start manipulating you. This process may seem deep, but it will be just the surface work that they do. Later when they know you're more comfortable, they reveal their true nature and start being dismissive and will stop paying attention, especially when you bring up your issues, needs and boundaries. You can try bringing it up and negotiating when it comes to providing you more attention and not dismissing you. Nevertheless, if you're dealing with a narcissistic individual, they might turn it around and pretend nothing bad is happening. You need to leave if nothing changes.

☞ Taking you away from your social circle AKA social abuse.
They might start with being charming but will gradually try to turn you against your loved ones. They don't do this in an obvious manner. Their efforts to get to know your family and friends are insincere. Some may even try to persuade you to leave to another city or a suburb so that it's more difficult for you to see your social circle. Of course they would use an excuse such as having a better quality home, or them being closer to their work. If someone goes miles to cause turmoil in your social life, they most likely are well aware of what they are doing, I recommend leaving them.

☞ Not sharing vulnerable things about their psyche.
They might create an illusion of sharing and closeness but will never get into their true emotions. Or they use that information to make you feel connected to them and bring it up often to explain their dysfunctional

behaviors. They might want to evoke guilt and shame in you through reminding you about what they went through in life. You will also never know how much of it is true. The Avoidants also do not share much, but that's because they find it hard to acknowledge their needs and to be comfortable while sharing. You can try to inquire more about their past, or levels of anxiety when it comes to communication. But if they continue to be secretive, you might want to inform them that you need more vulnerability in order to progress into a relationship. Leave if there is no negotiation from their side.

☞ Malicious blaming.

One of many dysfunctional communication techniques that is not only used by narcissists is blaming. Most people have used this technique at some point, but it's perceived as "being just". There are instances where we need to point out bad behavior, but this needs to be done in good faith and followed by a possible solution. If you blame for the sake of not feeling guilty or to get your way, it becomes malicious blaming. Non-narcissists usually do it unknowingly and are driven by the need to place the blame somewhere. Narcissists on the other hand know exactly what they are doing and use this technique to confuse their victims and make them feel bad. You won't achieve anything on dates or in a relationship if you point fingers at each other. You might be doing it subconsciously to protect yourself; this type of pattern can also be changed. Nevertheless, if you use blame maliciously to shame someone or control them, you're in the narcissistic ballpark. If you cannot comprehend that this behavior is wrong, doesn't serve you and needs to be changed, there's not much that can help you communicate. If your date in the early stages is already pointing a finger at you whenever there's a small hiccup, you're seeing a red flag.

☞ Emotional blackmail and playing the victim.

They will use emotional language against you. Non-narcissists also do it but unconsciously and out of desperation. Highly Preoccupied types can resort to this strategy as well when they feel that the relation is in jeopardy. Narcissists will know exactly what they're doing and how to push your emotional buttons. They might question your love for them and your intentions to have it their way. It goes side by side with gaslighting. You can bring this behavior to their attention and enquire for change. If the person acknowledges your point and promises change, this red flag could be bleached. One of my dates was very often bringing up a situation where their friend died in their arms. I was sympathetic at first but then I could see that he was using this story to get me to stop asking him difficult questions and to be more compliant.

REFLECTION

If you encounter a person with narcissistic tendencies, run. Nevertheless, narcissism is a spectrum; a lot of people may display some behaviors and traits while still being able to connect with others and have fulfilling relationships if they work on themselves through introspection and self-reflection. You can possibly try implementing boundaries, make requests, and call this person out, but you also need to recognize when the situation is unsalvageable. Treating narcissistic tendencies is very difficult because the person needs to understand that they have an issue, and this realization is not frequent in people who are highly self-centered. It's awesome to think of yourself as a god, why would you want to stop? The motivation would need to be your relationship and the need to become a better person. Most of the issues outlined above are deep rooted which is why my main advice is to cut contact with these types of people.

Highly Avoidant Red Flags

The list below reviews red flags of highly avoidant individuals. It will help you recognize those bad signs in others and also to assess if you display those behaviors. This list doesn't mean that you, as a somewhat Avoidant type, cannot have a healthy relationship. If you perform such behaviors, it might be time to address your behavioral patterns. As long as you do the work and watch out for your avoidant Part, you can create meaningful relationships. I've also included some ideas for you in case you meet a person that you really like but they display the behaviors listed below. Sometimes it's possible to negotiate some terms with your date and bleach this red flag. Please, remember that therapy is the best remedy for problematic attachment style.

☞ Withdrawing during conversations and changing subjects.
This is a behavior also present in narcissists. However, you can watch out for an embarrassed look on the face of the person to distinguish avoidance from lack of care. Avoidant people withdraw to protect themselves from strong emotions. They're unused to being vulnerable or they might believe that they don't have needs. You can try pointing the behavior out to your date in a curious way rather than in accusatory one and reassure them that you are here to find a solution. It can sometimes be remedied by soothing techniques, communication tactics and consistent effort. Although if the person is unwilling to work on it and deflects, then it might be best to move on and find a more suitable date.

☞ Sporadic contact and lack of initiation.
Narcissists might play games of pushing and pulling; an Avoidant will be consistently withdrawn especially when you have more needs for intimacy and closeness. In some cases, you might be able to negotiate some terms like agreement on the number of invitations per week, considerate texts, planning new activities, etc. You can obviously alternate between them, but Avoidants need more structure and planning in this department than Secure or Preoccupied individuals. If your date is unwilling to come on board in any capacity, you're barking up the wrong tree. If you're thinking that it's too early to make "demands", think of it as a request. They can obviously say "no", but then you might need to take steps to protect yourself and leave the situation because of it. They should have a choice whether to keep dating you and grant your request or stick to their old ways without you. Wait a few dates before requesting more effort from your date but if it starts to bother you emotionally, it's good to discuss it.

☞ Confused about their emotions towards you
They might show you some affection, especially in the beginning. But the connection will be inconsistent. That is because they get overwhelmed by their emotions easily. During childhood, they didn't develop good boundaries because they didn't believe their needs mattered. Being close and vulnerable seems unsafe because they are not used to it.

☞ Blaming people when they are trying to get close to them
This comes with a lack of boundaries. They develop a subconscious belief that there is nothing to be done apart from resenting others and ultimately loosening the bonds with people. They feel trapped and that their independence is in jeopardy.

☞ Not believing that they are good enough
Avoidant people usually have low self-esteem and don't believe that they "can give you want you want" because they don't measure up. No one's needs can be met 100% and at all times. Avoidants, however, didn't develop good communication and negotiation skills to be able to manage their and other's needs.

☞ Performing people-pleasing behaviors
A tactic that Avoidant people often develop is people pleasing. During their childhood that could have been the only way to avoid conflict. This type of person will not raise concerns with you because they are terrified of conflict.

☞ Commitment issues
Any signs of commitment and furthering the relation will scare them. Even though at their core they want closeness.

REFLECTION:
Avoidants can still have good relationships, but they need to work on their intimacy skills. They mostly do not have malicious intent, but their

way to self-soothe and to be in a relationship comes with withdrawal. You can work on it with them as you progress in your relationship, but if there's no progress, it's time to let go. To work on your avoidant behaviors, you will most likely need to address your childhood issues or traumas and mindfully restructure your behaviors. It will be worth it! If you do that you will gain deeper connections with people and your life can also become more fulfilling. You can heal in a secure relationship and with progressive sharing and experiencing conflict in a safe setting.

Red Flags in Highly Preoccupied People
Preoccupied individuals can be amazing partners. It's natural for them to be very caring, show emotions and to think about the well-being of the relationship. Nevertheless, if a person is very high on the preoccupation scale, this type can come with many toxic behaviors which can break the future relationship, even though the intent was the opposite. Here are some common red flags that could indicate that you're dating an individual with preoccupied attachment style.

☞ Not having any friends.
If this person doesn't have a circle of friends and isn't interested in getting one, it is a red flag. Often their preoccupation can go into love addiction (Mellody et al., 1992). Those individuals might put all their effort into one relationship and forsake any other social connections. Their partner becomes their whole world, only confidant, therapist, and outlet of emotions. That can be overbearing if they don't have proper boundaries. It can be helped but the Preoccupied needs to acknowledge their situation and make a conscious effort to work on their inner world and mechanisms. If it sounds like you, go back to Chapter 8: Social Skills Curriculum in Part 1 of the book and focus on those exercises and create your own steps to find your tribe before you engage in dating. Dating can be difficult at times; you need good people around you to talk to, hug or ask for advice. And once you've found your people, don't forget about them when you start dating or get into a relationship.

☞ Mindreading

I don't mean having psychic abilities but assuming you know what the other person is thinking. We all at times engage in mindreading, but, if someone is highly Preoccupied about their relationship, it magnifies. Mindreading can provoke strong emotions when we assume the worst. So, remember not to do it and if your date engages in it, bring it to their attention so that they can change as well.

☞ Excessive jealousy

It's common to get jealous sometimes, especially in polyamorous relationships. We like to be secure in the conviction that our partner cares and won't leave us. But high and frequent levels of jealousy are very toxic for the relationship. If your date is already displaying signs of controlling and possessive behaviors without reason, this can be a red flag. Ambiguous situations happen and our emotions might run high, but a good partner should be able to come to you with a concern and talk it out. Nevertheless, the beginning phase of dating entails that our date could potentially be seeing other people. Having a jealous feeling is okay, but if your date acts on it via interrogation, being outright angry at you or checking your phone without permission, it's not a good sign. Feelings and thoughts are not to blame but need to be accepted and processed. Acting out because of them, however, is problematic and needs to be stopped.

If you're a jealous type, you can work on yourself with introspection. Recognize your jealous Part, have an internal dialogue with it, do a reality check while you're at it. Consider if your jealousy is justified and what steps are appropriate.

You can call out your date on inappropriate behavior they displayed in front of you, for example flirting with another person while on a date with you. If you're not at the point of being able to request exclusivity, you can still request respect and acknowledgement. If someone chooses to go on a date with you, the commitment from both sides should be to give each other undivided attention for the duration of the date. Make sure to bring it to your date's attention firmly but kindly. But if you start making demands when it comes to exclusivity early on, it turns into toxic jealousy. Becoming exclusive and starting a relationship is a big commitment and should be discussed calmly and kindly by two consenting adults. If you're prone to misinterpret behaviors and jump to conclusions, make sure to account for that. Give your date the benefit of the doubt.

To avoid future misunderstandings, have a casual chat about what your date considers cheating. General ideas are not personal, you are not pointing a finger, but trying to get to know the person in front of you. For some people, cheating is only sex, but for another it will also be flirting and texting with other people who could be potential "threats."

If you want to process your jealousy with your date you can talk about a specific behavior that triggers you, perhaps because of your past experiences. Remember not to point a finger at them but at your feelings. Let them know how you feel when triggering behavior is performed and how they could help you not to feel that way, within reason. You can also acknowledge that you're aware that you're not an exclusive couple. Nevertheless, this doesn't mean that you can't ask for help. For example, you can ask your date to minimize time on their phone if you feel ignored and suspect that he or she is texting their other dates. As long as you're respectful, calm and reasonable with your requests you will not experience and act on toxic jealousy.

☞ Excessive neediness and clinginess

We all have needs that we want to fulfill through romantic relationships; that's the way to create deep bonds with someone. We need to put those needs in their hands, and they put theirs in ours, it sparks vulnerability and higher levels of connection and fulfillment. The problem begins when your partner is making demands instead of requests or their requests are humanly impossible to fulfill or cross over your boundaries. To address this, ask your friends for feedback when it comes to your needs. Make sure not to demand things but rather request them. Before you ask for something ask yourself: "is this request reasonable, doable and specific enough?" If it's connection that you want, give your date some options such as more texts or asking them to initiate meetings more frequently. You can even come up with frequency and timeline together if needed.

☞ Having a meaning in life only through romantic relationships
You don't have to be long around a person to establish if they have a tendency to do this. Watch out for the way they talk about their previous partners and about you. If there's nothing going on in their life apart from seeing you, it can be a red flag. Lack of hobbies, passions or career is unhealthy. It doesn't mean we have to have all the above plus heaps of meaningful friendships, but we should aspire to it. If your date has no interests or something to fill their life meaningfully, your relationship can become their only energy source. That can become toxic very quickly, especially if you want to take more time for yourself, your hobbies, and friends. This would need to be remedied by them practicing introspection and self-development to create a plan to get all of the mentioned fulfilling things.

☞ Intense tantrums and accusations.
Some highly Preoccupied people can give you a hard time if you don't meet their unrealistic needs. They will also hear your arguments as excuses without assessing if you might have a point. Tantrums, aggression, accusations, manipulation, and general mood destabilization can be their "go to" strategy. They lack healthy ways of communication and dealing with emotions so they might externalize them. Some of those tactics might be used by narcissistic types as well but their motivation is different. The Preoccupied want to desperately get their needs met and get closer to their partner. Unfortunately, this type of behavior will successfully drive people away whereas narcissists do it knowingly and from a superior position and don't care about closeness.

   A cure for this is inner work, soothing techniques, and appropriate Time Outs. Tantrums and blaming are toxic communication patterns that hide deeper emotions such as perceived lack of respect, attention or understanding. When you learn to find this deeper emotion that caused the tantrum, you'll need to also learn how to talk about it calmly. Talk about a specific problematic behavior that was triggering for you. Establish what deep emotions it made you feel and what you and the other person could do differently next time. Form a reasonable request and ask if this person is willing to grant you that need.

☞ Lack of external and internal boundaries

We already discussed how to create your own boundaries and why they're so important. We also need to recognize poor boundary setting skills in other people. People like that will be invading your emotional and personal space and will have also bad internal dialogues. Excessive neediness and clinginess are typical signs of lack of boundaries. Also, strong internalization of what other people say and do. You can call it child-like self-centered thinking and premonition that everything is their fault. The Preoccupied often alternates between blaming themselves and blaming other people. To work on your boundaries, return to Part 1 of the book.

OTHER RED FLAGS

☞ Not having boundaries with their parents

If your date is close with their parents, it can be an awesome green flag, however if they are too close, you'll never be number one. You shouldn't be competing for your future partner's affection with his or her parents. If they constantly bring up their mom or dad and base most of their opinions on what they believe, it might become a big issue. If your date seems to be enmeshed with one or both of their parents, don't recognize it and are unwilling to work on it, it can be a predictor of future issues.

If it sounds like you have this red flag, work on it by developing new boundaries with your parents. Think about what your parents can do or what you could do to make yourself more comfortable in the relationship between you and your parents. If you feel very comfortable with enmeshment but perhaps your past partners pointed out that there's an issue, it could be the time to reassess your parent/child relation.

☞ Peter Pan & Wendy's Syndrome

You know the story of Peter Pan and Wendy. They didn't grow up when in Neverland. That's how this name came about. Peter Pan's or Wendy's Syndrome is a situation when a person is not growing up emotionally and doesn't act their age.

Perhaps you met a super handsome guy who makes you laugh but is going out drinking five nights a week and will not have a grown-up conversation about feelings, needs and boundaries? That's him, your Peter Pan. Or maybe you went out with a girl that posts drunken selfies all over Instagram and will forget to respond to you. That's her, Wendy. People who find it hard to commit and display immaturity, seem locked at the age of 18. If it sounds like you, there's some growing up that you need to do before you start looking for a relationship. If you struggle to find motivation and a purpose create a list of your values and goals and follow them.

☞ Having multiple short lived and mostly sexual relationships with people
If a person moves very quickly from one person to the other and doesn't create any connection with you but is already asking for sex, you can suspect that they want a casual relationship. If you don't mind casual – that's great, go for it. But if you seek something long-term and meaningful, it's probably the time to let your date know that you're not the best fit. It's okay not to like casual relationships. Don't make yourself go into something that isn't in line with your values just because society says you should be fine with it.

If you find yourself in that description, it's best if you make it clear to your dates that you seek a purely casual relationship. If you're truly looking for a meaningful long-term relationship, however, it could be good to start with creating some connection with your date before getting sexual. There are exceptions to the rule, of course, and perhaps you'll find "the one" through a one-night stand. Nevertheless, I have also heard from many people that there's something that I call "the morning ick." The ick is when you've had sex with a person that you weren't connected to or attracted to. Perhaps there was too much alcohol and you both thought it was a great idea at the time, but you regret the decision in the morning. Some of the people that I heard that statement from added that their date was fairly attractive, but there wasn't enough time to connect. Alcohol and other drugs can create an illusion of connection.

We can often confuse this type of a person with someone that desperately wants connection and uses sex to gain it. Some people also reported to me that they want to "seal the deal" by having sex as soon as possible. This means they believe their date will develop feelings for them through sex. It might happen, but it's not how true connection is created. So, make sure that there's no bias in your mind about what sex is for you or other people. Sex should be a beautiful addition to a pre-existing connection. You can express and feel the connection while having sex.

☞ People who are emotionally draining

Those people are very depressing, critical, and draining. They don't contribute emotionally or in any other way to their relationships and friendships and often have issues of their own that are contributing to this emotional vampirism. They might not even realize that they drain their environment. If you feel depleted and lack energy after seeing this type of individual it might be a sign that you're dating someone who has poor boundaries. Conversations with them usually focus on them and on their problems or them needing help and support from you.

This type of person not only won't be a good partner, but they're also not great friends to have. They will only take and will never contribute to your life. Sometimes they might seemingly contribute by inviting you to a place, offering help, etc. Nevertheless, this help will be concentrated on them and their emotional needs that they will want you to address for them. I don't believe in absolute self-lessness, we need some reason and motivation to help, such as feeling better about ourselves or a sense of fulfillment. Nevertheless, people who behave like this will have a lot of external motives that don't include self-actualization but rather focus on their need for attention, and pity. If you find yourself in that description, it would be best if you engaged in therapy to address your issues and learn to be more self-sufficient.

☞ People who demand things

Your date doesn't need to be a Narcissist or Preoccupied to demand things. If someone makes big requests without giving you the option to back out or make it very difficult for you to say "no", it's not the best sign. Make sure that you're not a demander. If your date is one, remember to bring this up and discuss the difference between requests and demands. When you request things, people can naturally accept or deny the request; to demand is more absolute.

Use boundaries and create consequences for people that do not respect them and that can include ceasing contact with them. That's much better than demanding things from unwilling people.

☞ People who use aggression or have poor emotional control

Any displays of aggressive behaviors towards you or other people are red flags, this will include:

- raising their voice in aggression without being provoked or with minimal provocation.
- breaking things.
- stopping you from freely moving your body
- painful or uncomfortable touch that they do not perceive as out of line even though you expressed it's problematic.

A good negotiator and communicator will keep calm even during provocations. We cannot explain those behaviors as a "temperament". People can have big personalities and have short tempers, but this can be addressed with proper communication skills and inner soothing.

There's no excuse for aggression and uncontained anger, especially during the initial dating period. We all have moments of weakness in critical situations, but if the person can't contain themselves in simple moments or in the presence of others, it's never a good sign.

☞ People who show contempt towards others

People who show signs of contempt towards you and others won't make great partners. If your date rolls their eyes at you, ridicules your point of view consistently or shuts you down before you can finish a sentence, they will most likely continue to do so.

If you realize that you perform such behaviors, it's time to stop, especially when it comes to the people closest to you. It will definitely not deepen your relationships but destroy them. Catch yourself in a contemptuous mode and ask this contempt Part of you to step back. Put yourself in the shoes of the person in front of you, make room for their opinion. You don't have to judge them, just listen, and consider. You will meet many people who will be different from you and it's a good skill to still be able to relate to them on some level and accept their differences. It doesn't mean that you agree with their values or opinions, but you create space to share.

☞ People who get defensive and deflect

These people will have problems with internalizing blame and will try to shift it quickly on to you, or someone or something else. A cure to defensiveness can be practicing not placing the blame on anyone. If you need to blame something, you can blame the problem itself, but it's best if you switch into solution mode.

Instead of blaming people for their emotions, reactions and issues, ask: "How can I make the situation better?" If the other person is not outright rude or performing any other toxic behaviors, there's no need for you to defend yourself. A lot of people can be defensive if they feel attacked, but if someone's only response is defense, they should address this pattern. If your date doesn't see an issue with their defensiveness and is unwilling to address it, you will be signing up for a toxic pattern in your future relationship with that person. If you find that defensiveness is your frequent response, you can also try to take some responsibility for whatever happened and see how it feels. It doesn't mean that you're a bad person but consider what needs to change in the future when it comes to your behavior. Abstaining from defensiveness allows you to problem solve much better and more quickly.

☞ People who criticize themselves and others

These are people who find issues with everything; negativity floats right out of them. You will rarely hear a compliment from a critic. Most times, however, you will hear what is wrong. Being overly critical is a control mechanisms like perfectionism, people pleasing or micromanagement. Critics think that if they criticize others or themselves enough, it will somehow improve the situation. On the same level it can be a manifestation of care but also perceived lack of control. If you're exposed to continuous criticism, you may become critical as well. We often take on mindset of our partners and even if we are mindful it can be very draining to avoid starting to be critical towards others and yourself.

If your date has an inner critic, it's not as invasive for you but it means that the self-esteem of that person is not in the best shape. Low self-worth can spill over to relationships because it makes us less mindful, connected, and self-assured. People who are more confident in themselves make better decisions and lead happier lives; they can share this mindset and emotions with others. Therefore, people with good levels of self-esteem make better partners.

The best solution for easing up your critic is to replace your critical thoughts with something objective or positive or to take action and change the situation to the point where you're happy with an outcome and you can accept unchangeable drawbacks. True change will come with learning how to accept imperfections that are outside of our control. You may be thinking that you need your critic to motivate you to succeed or be better. Take it from a therapist that helped many people calm their critic Parts, it will not make you a lesser person, but it will open your eyes to the good things in life and help you enjoy life rather than looking for yet another negative thing. You can speak to yourself with compassion and kindness and still achieve success and feel motivated. Your values, goals and loved ones need to become your future motivation.

☞ People who use passive aggression

If your date expresses microaggressions or uses tactics like the silent treatment or withholding affection, you're not on a path to a healthy relationship together. Sarcasm and jokingly insulting you are also passive aggressive behaviors. If it sounds like something that you did in your previous relationships, stop. These types of behaviors will not lead you to what you want from the other person but rather will put you on the fast track to resentment and further damage this relationship. You need to be mindful of when you are being emotional underneath. If you're feeling angry, spiteful, unfulfilled, or needing something from your date, most likely your passive aggressive behaviors will follow. Acknowledge which of your needs are unmet and look for healthy ways to fulfill them. To do that use healthy communication strategies and soothing tactics.

☞ People who try to control others

Narcissists will try to control you so that they can have power over you. Preoccupied types will want to control so that you won't leave them. Whatever reason your date has for controlling behaviors, they're unhealthy. Many people can be somewhat controlling at times but that can be remedied by an honest conversation and a plan for the future. Talk about why your date is trying to control the situation and how you can help within reason. If your controlling date can't handle this type of conversation, you might need to let them go. And if you have a controller Part, make sure to acknowledge it, listen to its needs and find healthier ways to fulfill them or try therapy.

☞ People who have trust issues

Usually, this type will have bad past experiences in their relationships. Those past events might have hardened their hearts. Just because someone had a bad past doesn't not give them a free pass to accuse you. They're often from the Preoccupied part of society. If your date starts to bring lack of trust into your relationship, you need to voice it in order to see if it's reparable. Very often, if you support your new partner where appropriate, they might develop trust towards you.

To establish what is "appropriate" you'll need to have an honest conversation about how your new partner would like to be supported in their difficult emotions and what you're willing to give. The plan can be temporary or long term if the ideas are not too invasive. If you can find a middle ground for a pathway towards trust, you can still develop a healthy relationship in the future.

However, if your date believes that he or she is beyond repair and isn't interested in therapy or at least having conversations about the issue, then you don't have many prospects for a relationship. I often hear from the trusting partner: "Why should I do anything? I'm trustworthy!". Yes, you might be and the untrusting person often knows it. Nevertheless, it's not about you, but about the psyche of the person with trust issues. So, acknowledge that it has nothing to do with you and establish how much support you're willing to give. Use this mindset with jealousy as well. For example, if for some reason your date gets jealous, suspicious or doesn't trust you with something, the deal between you can be that the untrusting brings it up, the trusting gives the untrusting a hug and you both talk about it when you're alone.

☞ People who don't accept other's opinions and act ignorant
This type will talk to you as long as you confirm their opinions about the world. Nevertheless, if you deviate from their script, they will lose interest in a conversation or even show displeasure that you have another take on the matter. There are no two identical people with the same knowledge and opinions. The quicker we accept it, the less discord there will be in the world.

You need a partner that is somewhat different from you so that you can debate and exchange information and make things interesting. A date that not only doesn't want to hear you out but is dismissive, sarcastic, and evasive will probably use similar tactics in the future. People whose Love Style is intellectual, especially, can suffer if they choose a partner like this. Your opinions will not be heard or respected, and you will start to feel disconnected and resentful. You need to negotiate a behavior change with your date. Often people who cannot listen to other perspectives have problems with boundaries, especially internal ones. They might feel that different opinions impede their worldviews, something which would need to be addressed with inner work and therapy.

☞ People with addiction issues

If your date shows signs of substance use or has any other addictive tendences, it's a red flag. At first it can be difficult to establish if it's an addiction, but some questions about frequency of partying and meeting your date's friends can help you to discover deeper issues. Of course, you don't want to interrogate; questions need to be posed in a casual manner. For example: "Seems like you know a lot of cool bars! Do you go out every weekend?" Small talk and keeping it casual is the key. Make your date feel comfortable and be curious and the red and green flags will pop up by themselves. If, however, your date comes to you with information that they're in recovery, that's great but make sure to enquire for how long they've been clean.

Dating an addict and then going into a relationship with one is not a great idea. It obviously depends on the scale and type of addiction. Remember that addiction doesn't only mean drugs, gambling, sex, or porn. Compulsive and disconnecting behavior disguising as productivity is workaholism. You might be thinking that your date is so ambitious and hard working, when it's a coping mechanism that helps them with internal issues in a psychologically dysfunctional but moneywise functional way. The problem is that you'll never be a priority in their life. This person could meet a supermodel that they feel great about and very often addiction would win anyway. Human beings need a balance between social life and career. If it's not there, it stops being healthy for them and the people around them.

Addiction equals disconnection from the real world. Addicted people feel connected only when they perform addictive behavior which means that healthy things are not as appealing to them anymore (Wilson, 2015). They also reinforce it through repetition and that messes up their dopamine system. When an addictive behavior is performed it creates such a big spike of dopamine that other things in life can't measure up.

The real-world stops being appealing. A person stops enjoying and starts to compulsively "want". Addicts body stops producing dopamine by itself because it was given so much of the unhealthy stimuli.

As a person who works with addicts, I can say that addictions often come in clusters, which means that if addicts come to me with sex addiction, they often have other addictions. If someone has a strongly addictive personality, they might quickly fall into another addiction. It's not a rule, but people with single addictions find it much easier to overcome temptations.

It's up to you to decide if you wish to date someone in recovery, but here is some valuable information. Many addiction programs suggest that participants avoid dating or entering relationships for at least a year after they get sober. Therefore, make sure that your date is a long-term success story before you get serious. And even if your partner is in recovery, it could be good to look into programs like Al-Anon that help families of Alcoholics.

You also need to remember that addiction comes with lying and deceit. Many addicts will be good people who feel very guilty for the harm they cause to others. Even though they have the best of intentions and at the core they're decent human beings, it's often not enough to overcome the addiction. At their worst, people can get very manipulative, aggressive, and deceitful all in the name of the drug. So be sure to weigh all the pros and cons if you want to date a recovering addict.

☞ People who don't commit to things and "flake out" on you
Another red flag is flakiness. If your date treats you like "an option", that's a bad sign. We obviously have a big pool of options, but we don't have to be nasty to others. When you go out on a date, be fully present. If you make plans, keep your promise to that person or inform them in advance that you won't make it. If you feel that there's a better option which just came up, it's not the best to keep leading on others. If you don't stand by your word, you don't look good to anyone. You want a partner with a strong moral compass; someone who knows how to decide and stick

with his or her beliefs. Only this way you can be relatively sure of their loyalty and devotion to you in the future. If your date already has a habit of blowing off plans that they made with you and isn't attentive on dates, they won't make a good partner.

I had a client tell me about a man she met just one time, she gave me permission to discuss this story. He came clean with her about being involved with another woman who was perhaps leaving the country. He was currently looking for new options, for when and if his current partner left. Now think if you would like to be that other woman possibly leaving the country and your partner is already looking around. He did come clean, but he keeps his current partner in the dark. Just because he came clean doesn't make this behavior moral or good and you don't want an immoral partner. You want someone with principles, not a flake. Someone that will support you through tough times and not escape the moment the fun is interrupted.

☞ People who haven't addressed their past trauma

Trauma can come from childhood, past relationships, accidents, or other unforeseen tragedies. Untreated trauma or other mental health issues can easily spill into relationships. A person can have amazing potential as a partner, but if they have an untreated condition, it will affect your relationship at some point.

That's why talking about the past is so important. If you see that your date is avoiding such conversations or has very strong reactions to those topics, you can suspect that something is going on. People with trauma have very poor emotional regulation, are susceptible to addictions and dysfunctional behavior patterns. The person might not even realize that the trauma is there because they use masking behaviors such as inner criticism, addictions, or pretending that the past doesn't matter. Traumatized people will have a different sense of reality and find it hard to connect with others. Escaping from emotions will be the most important thing and connection will be too scary and confronting for them. If you or date have such issues, I highly recommend getting professional help. You will greatly improve your quality of life if you take this step.

☞ People who cheated on their partners before

A history of cheating on partners is also not the best sign. There's a saying "once a cheater, always a cheater." I don't believe it's true in every case. People may have different reasons for cheating and if they change their situation, mindset, and/or a partner, it might not happen again. For example, if someone was young at the time and didn't know any better and then went through major events in their life that altered their values and views, they might have been transformed.

People often engage in cheating when they don't see a way out. We should be choosing to be with one another everyday instead of "locking ourselves in." Humans don't do very well when free will is taken away. So don't treat your relationships like cages but more like a home that you chose to come back to because it's great and the way you like it. If your partner knows that there's no way you'll ever leave even if they do horrible things, you lose all the leverage that helps you keep a balanced relationship.

We label cheaters very strongly and scrutinize them, but we forget that 50% of people in committed relationships and 20% of married people cheated at some point and that's only the official statistics (Rosenberg, 2018). I very much doubt all respondents were truthful and that all the cheaters were begging to answer that question. Around 90% of people never find out about their partner's affair.

In saying this, I don't want to sound like I give away free passes for cheating. Cheating is a nasty thing to do to your partner; it hurts a lot and not only the betrayed but the whole family if there is one. Nevertheless, affairs are very common. It's very easy to cheat, especially nowadays. The question is why wouldn't you cheat? And we come back to moral principles. So, if your partner is a moral, sexual addiction-free person, it's possible they will be loyal.

I encourage couples to talk openly about past infidelity, what it meant for your partner and why it wouldn't happen again. Make sure that there are plenty of reasons not to cheat. If you work on your relationship together, you have a good chance at loyal companionship. Even if there was no past infidelity, it's crucial to discuss what cheating is for each of the partners. One person accepts it if their partner flirts with another person and another won't. So, make sure you're on the same page. If you make it easy for one another to talk about difficult thoughts or urges, it's much less likely that one of you will feel the need to cheat.

Nevertheless, there are types of compulsive cheaters who can be fueled by narcissism and a sense of entitlement because of sex addiction or both. Sexual addictions are one of the hardest to overcome. That's why to avoid this type of person you need to first screen for narcissistic behaviors and rule out addictions. If those two don't come into the picture and your date seems to be reformed for a long time, there's still a good chance that he or she will be a loyal partner. Make sure to address the topic of infidelity before you talk about getting serious and starting a committed relationship.

I know I pointed out a lot of things and different perspectives when it comes to cheating. It can be confusing for you if past infidelity is or isn't a red flag. That's because it's a controversial and complicated topic. This can be a red flag if a person is not reformed, acts entitled, or is not working on their sex addiction. But if we pointed a finger every time someone with a history of infidelity comes along, we would be ruling out over a half of population. You'll need to make up your own mind about it. It's alright if you do want to rule out anyone who cheated, perhaps this is your boundary and a dealbreaker. Cheating is not a very courageous thing to do. Open communication about the problems like lack of sexual or mental fulfillment in a relationship is much more Adult-like.

REFLECTION

These are the most common categories of red flags that stand from attachment styles, bad communication patterns and/or trauma. I realize that you might see some of them in yourself and your loved ones. It's never too late to change your ways to achieve better communication skills and emotional regulation and therefore enable yourself to handle conflict and build healthy future relationships.

If you want a great partner, you need to become a great partner. Excuses such as: "My date should just like me the way I am", don't apply. That's something dysfunctional communicators tell themselves to avoid making an effort. Your bad communication is not who you are at the core. At the core we are our values and principles that we create to lead a healthy and fulfilled life. Passivity, aggression, sarcasm, blaming, criticism and all the others are not values. Therefore, by changing these patterns of behavior you're not disposing of who you are as a person but enabling yourself to connect to others in a more meaningful and healthy way.

As functional adults we should be acting with courage, calmness, and curiosity. This is you at the core, so get off your butt and work on your communication, behaviors, boundaries, attachment style and insecurities so you do not display those red flags to your dates or to anyone else.

Don't just let things continue for weeks if you see that there's something wrong and your date doesn't want to talk about it or acknowledge it. If there's no plan for change, leave and spare yourself the difficulties of a breakup. Even though I gave some solutions and antidotes to red flags, please remember that you can't "fix" people. All you can do is make requests and if the person follows through and wants to work with you, only then there's hope. It's more about their willingness and actions rather than about you. Your only options, in this order, are honest conversations, putting in boundaries, making requests, informing that person about the consequences of their behaviors, and leaving the relationship.

What not to do when you're dating a person with red flags?

☞ Being the best you can for them so that the person falls for you and changes. They won't because they're too comfortable. If you pretend and play to their whims, you'll be stuck in that situation.

☞ Becoming "fake distant" so that they see how much they want you and they start trying. If you come back each time because they've made a tiny, irrelevant and short-lasting change, you're solidifying their belief that they only have to pretend to change.

☞ **Leaving but not emotionally.** If you decide to cut the contact, do it properly. If you hold on emotionally so that "one day you'll be reunited and your situationship will become a serious committed relationship" you're clinging to an outlandish fairy tale that will only hurt you. There's nothing healthy about holding on. If it really is meant to be, it would need to happen with a different mindset and context. Both of you would need to let go and decide to come back with a new outlook on things and that will only happen when you leave physically and emotionally.

REFLECTION

Please spare yourself heartache and replace those strategies with working on your self-esteem, good boundaries, requesting respect and handling breakups and rejections. Having those in place will get you the best possible matches. A quality person will look for a quality partner. Insecurity, manipulation and hanging around when you're unwanted doesn't exactly scream "quality!"

So, make sure you master recognizing red flags. This takes practice and mindfulness. Make sure that you do the Mindful Check-Ins and stay centered during dates. Stop yourself from creating fairy tales and focus on what your date is doing and saying and if those actions and words match. Saying does not equal doing, therefore, focus on consistency, quality, and quantity of green and red flags. If you know that some things like kissing, alcohol, sex, or compliments cloud impair your judgement, make sure to be extra cautious about those factors. You might want to stay very mindful during or after situations infused with physical or sexual connection. It's easy to float away on that cloud to a land where you have a house together with a white picket fence and a dog.

Understand Your General Dealbreakers

General dealbreakers are kinds of red flags that don't mean that there is anything wrong with the person that we are dating, but we don't seem to fit when it comes to some important areas of life, and nothing can be done about it. They usually pop up when it comes to values and choosing a joint path as a couple. To understand your general dealbreakers, please perform the following exercise.

* * *

EXERCISE: Recognize Your Dealbreakers by Using Your Values
Complete the exercise depending on what you value the most in life. Rate each of the categories listed below from 1 to 10. Don't overthink it, as there are no wrong answers. This is simply a graphic representation of your priorities.
- Spirituality –
- Money and Finances –
- Career and Work –
- Personal Growth and Learning –
- Partner and Love –
- Family and Friends –
- Community –
- Environment –
- Fun and Recreation –
- Health and Fitness –
- Politics and World Situation –

Your prospective partner's answers should look somewhat similar if you are truly compatible. That is why you need to assess if they have any dealbreakers when it comes to incompatible values. Write down what those dealbreakers are. Think about who your prospective partner needs to be, what they want in life and what values they are cultivating. Make sure that your dealbreakers are things that you truly cannot look past. You don't want every one of your whims to become a dealbreaker, because it will be very hard for you to find a suitable partner. We often focus on trivial issues such as attractiveness, the partner's charisma, their wealth, or their style, instead of paying attention to crucial views and values compatibility. Think about things that your "soul" couldn't stand in a long-term relationship. Also, you might not realize that some issues will affect your relationship in the future, so take into account that you might be wrong.

Examples of common dealbreakers:
- One of the partners wants to have a family in the future and the other one doesn't.
- Having different ideas about finances and building wealth in the future.
- Having different religions or spiritual beliefs.
- Having different ideas on what life is about. (E.g., If your partner is into fitness and spends all their free time at the gym and you want more couple's time and you believe that love is more important.)
- Differences in how you want to raise your children in the future and how you want to run the household.
- Differences in political views.
- Differences in medical views. (E.g., In recent years people started being mindful about their partner's vaccination status. Some will not date a partner who is vaccinated with the Covid-19 vaccine, and some will not have relationship with an unvaccinated person.)
- Differences in sexual drive and need for physical intimacy and receiving affection.

* * *

SUMMARY

In this chapter we discussed a variety of red flags that you can find in people. We started with the most prevalent extreme and abusive behaviors that you need to watch out for, because people who perform them can be very dangerous. Next, I outlined narcissistic red flags that are also crucial to recognize. It's not uncommon for narcissistic people to be also physically and psychologically abusive. Next, we delved into red flags of highly

Avoidant individuals and highly anxiously attached people. Lastly, I've described other common bad signs to watch out for. This chapter also gives you some ideas on how to improve those areas if you see them in yourself and how to negotiate change with your date. I introduce the idea of using your healthy boundaries and good communication to bleach the red flags to yellow and possibly even make them disappear. This will happen only if your date has the willingness to change and make things work. Cutting ties is the only option if your date has no intention to change and work on themselves. I've outlined what not to do when you see some prominent red flags. Lastly, we discussed general dealbreakers and how to recognize them using our own values.

Chapter 19:
Green Flags and Final Accounting

Now that you have an idea about what to avoid, you can focus on what you do want in your partner. Go back to your Perfect Partner List, as it will help you recognize these qualities via your date's behaviors. If you want a green flag partner, you'll also need to display those. This chapter will talk about positive signs in potential partners but will also motivate you to display those behaviors yourself. Inner work and becoming the best possible partner will give you good ideas on what to look for and won't allow you to settle for less. Displaying those behaviors will make you realize that you're not asking for too much! We already discussed red flags and if they can be "bleached to yellow" Meaning, if the red flags can be changed and worked on and how. After we get to know the green flags, I'll also include an exercise that will help you in analyzing the green, yellow, and red flags ratio in your future dates. This will give you a better idea about your future with that person.

☞ Being generous.

We already discussed generosity as a quality that every good partner should have. Remember to be generous in different ways such as with your time, effort, finances, physical touch, and support. It will greatly depend on your date's Love Style/Language. So initiate dates and plan for them. Remember what your date has shared with you and bring it up in conversations where appropriate. Offer to pay for something or offer a sympathetic ear or some advice. You can also send your date a considerate text to show that you think about them. Any small kindness can be a sign of generosity.

Be careful not to brag about how generous you are. If someone is using their generosity as a weapon to show how good they are, it stops being generosity and becomes a red flag. But remember not to over give. If you don't see reciprocation, stop giving.

☞ Adding value to your life

Other people's good behavior, values, moral compass, skills, and knowledge will rub off on us. It's a green flag with a broad range of options for behaviors. It taps into what generosity is, but it expands to this person's influence on us. For example, it has been proven that if we're around people who are productive and successful, we become more successful ourselves (Maxwell, 2009). Or, if we spend a lot of time with good communicators, we're much more likely to communicate better in the future. If you feel that your date has a good influence on you, it's a green flag. They can enhance your life. If you're feeling that you only give and do not get anything in return or that you need to carry the whole relationship, it's a bad sign. Evaluate if your date has strengths and see how those strengths can contribute to your life in the future. Maybe your date is funny, conscientious, or knowledgeable in some areas and you lack some skills when it comes to those topics. Those skills can be practiced and learned; your date can be your role model. And you can share your expertise.

☞ Showing interest in your family and friends

I'm not talking about dying to meet everyone after a second date but your date should at least show some interest in the friendships that you have with other people. When you do introduce your date to your friends and family, that's when the true test begins. It can be quite confronting to meet friends and especially your date's relatives, but if you want to show you care, you will put in the effort to make some kind of connection with each person.

You don't have to become best friends with everyone, but some small talk should be required. If you're an antisocial person and you find it hard, think of it as something that needs to be done and push yourself to make an effort. That's what you need to do if you want to show true interest in your date. Sometimes it can be a great experience, but most people will get a bit nervous before meeting their date's significant others. Think of it as a gift that you give to your date.

☞ Keeping the connection going

Later it becomes easier to connect because you know each other better, but at the beginning, even the best couple might have awkward moments. A person who truly cares will make sure that there's something to bond over. If they feel that the topic is coming to an end, they'll come up with a new one. If your date is withdrawn, or looks towards their phone or watch, it's not the best sign. Of course, some people will do it from anxiety, but I would suggest telling your date about it or at least "faking it until you make it." If you're acting withdrawn without giving a reason, you will be giving off an "uninterested" vibe. If, however, you can't stop yourself from withdrawing behaviors, let your date know that you're stressed and it's your comfort mechanism. If someone likes you, they'll appreciate the honesty and, if he or she is looking down on you because of it, it's probably not a good match anyway.

☞ Being vulnerable and sharing things when appropriate.

You should be looking for a wholehearted person with no ulterior motives. This person will not use you as an outlet for negative emotions and flood you with too much personal information. That person will listen to your story and share some personal things where appropriate so that you can bond. Being vulnerable in front of a new person isn't easy, so if your date doesn't mind sharing it also speaks volumes about their courage. Remember not to confuse vulnerability with weakness. Naivety, oversharing and trusting without basis for trust is a weakness. Vulnerability comes when you know a bit more about the world and how hurtful it can get, but you choose to be vulnerable anyway. That takes courage and being comfortable with sometimes getting rejected.

☞ Showing up
If the person that you are dating shows up for you consistently, it's a green flag. If they do need to postpone the meeting, they'll do it in a kind and timely manner. They will set up a new date and will try to make it up to you in some way.

Sounds simple, but it's not for some people. If your date constantly postpones date plans and misses some events that are important to you, it's a massive red flag. So, automatically showing up and being consistent will be your green flag.

☞ Good communication patterns and staying calm in a conflict.
Everyone needs a stable partner who can withstand conflict and arrive at a solution. If your date is calm and composed during stressful situations and deep conversations, it's a great sign. A person with good communication patterns will not blame you or themselves. They will talk about their own emotions without making you feel that you caused them. They will talk about behaviors that you or other people perform rather than attack your character. They might ask you to change certain behaviors calmly and politely but firmly, obviously within reason. They might even enquire about your feelings and needs. Their requests will mostly be formed in a specific and timely way so that it's easy for other people to fulfill them. So, make sure to practice good communication and emotional regulation.

☞ Being consistent with good behaviors
Make sure that the person that you're dating exhibits good behavior often and consistently. This will show you that they have a pattern rather than occasional enlightenment. That's how you know if a person is stable and will not surprise you with a 180-degree turn. We obviously grow and self-actualize over time, but we don't become dramatically different overnight either. If your date is inconsistent in what they're doing and saying, it's a bad sign. If there's no consistency, you can suspect hidden narcissism or some mental health problems or simply lack of interest. Look for

people who follow through with what they say and show you the regularity in their qualities over time. This includes consistency in showing up, displays of affection for you and in behavior towards other people.

If your date is mostly composed but throws a tantrum or gets aggressive or possessive from time to time, this doesn't just get erased by their mostly good behavior. I heard multiple times from people who were or still are in abusive relationships: "My partner is mostly calm except for the times when he/she breaks things or gets obsessively jealous. But apart from that he/she is great."

It doesn't work like this. We face many difficult situations, and everyone can have a breakdown when there's a lot of turmoil on the horizon, but that might happen once every blue moon, not every month or week. If you see that there's a pattern, it stops being a rare occasion and starts to be abusive.

☞ Having a balanced life
A partner who has a balanced and healthy life will be an awesome asset. It might sound a bit calculated but if you don't do the math you might end up with someone who brings you down. If your date seems to have a flourishing career, social life, and healthy lifestyle, it's definitely a green flag. It means that they will bring that health into a prospective relationship with you. People with lives like this are also on average better communicators as they know how to soothe themselves and have a support network and purpose in life. Living healthily brings joy that you can share with other people.

☞ Listening actively and asking insightful questions.
The true test when it comes to listening is passed with time. If your date listened actively to what you've said about yourself, they might bring up this information in future conversations. Also, if your date elaborates on your story, enquires about it and stays on topic, it means that they're attentive and interested. If your date, on the other hand, is only nodding and skipping from topic to topic so that they can suit their own

preferences, it's not the best sign. A date who asks good questions is a blessing. Not only does it take the pressure away from you, it also is a very good sign. It shows that the other person is actively interested in you and wants to build up their understanding of you.

☞ Being respectful and considerate

Even if your date displays many great green flags, if this one is missing you should move on and keep looking! Respect and thoughtfulness shouldn't be only displayed towards you, but to other people, especially older people. If your date is disrespectful on a regular basis, I wouldn't be surprised if they eventually start being like this to you. If you hear that your date is talking in a disrespectful way about their parents, friends, or ex partners without major reasons like abuse, it's a massive red flag.

So, make sure that your date is a respectful person. It can be as simple as opening a door for a girl, pushing the chair back for her, getting the first drink, or checking in with your date, for example, asking if they're comfortable in the venue. You can also think of practical things like bringing water to your table. Those small acts of kindness show that you're putting in some effort already. It's profitable in many different areas to be considerate and thoughtful. Obviously, pay attention if people are reciprocating, but sharing in that way will quickly bring you allies.

☞ You feel like you can be your true and best self around that person.

If you feel that you don't have to pretend or tiptoe around your date, it's an amazing sensation. If they appreciate your sense of humor, quirks and are happy to hear your opinions even if they have different ones, that's also a good sign. If you feel constantly alert and afraid that they will criticize you or look at you funny, you're probably not the best match. This green flag unfortunately can't be worked on or improved. You either fit or you don't. Don't try to force this type of connection. It's okay to not fit in. You won't like everyone on this planet and not everyone will enjoy spending time with you either. So, let's accept it and go back to your search.

☞ Being comfortable talking about emotions and difficult topics
Being able to handle emotions is a part of good communication. The more the person is able to soothe themselves, the more they'll be able to hold space for you and support you. Tough discussions can trigger even the best communicators. Make sure that your date is able to self-regulate and to be there for you emotionally when you're in need. As long as you're both able to alternate with emotional support when needed, it shows compatibility. This isn't easy to establish in early dating, so keep an eye out for this one after going into a relationship too.

☞ Being highly self-aware
Intrapersonal knowledge is very important. If you're clear about what's going on inside of you, you can interact with the world in the very best way possible. Managing what's going on inside makes you a better partner. People who are like this know what they want and how to get it. The path and goals are clear for them. It also means that, if they decide to get into a relationship with you, they are less likely to just turn around and leave, because they know they've made the right choice. Those individuals will also be self-actualized and happy with who they are, so you don't have to fear the 180-degree change happening a few months into a relationship. Being in touch with your emotions, challenging yourself, trying new things, and working on your communication will all help you achieve better self-awareness. And if your date shows you that they work on self-actualizing as well, it's a big green flag.

☞ Being empathetic.
You need to know that your partner will be there for you. Empaths can be the best partners who will know when something is off and will want to support you through tough times in your life. You need someone who will care for you and the other people in your life. If you plan to create a family in the future, empathy is a crucial component that you should be looking for in a partner. Parenting requires a lot of devotion, hard work, and emotional regulation. Empathy is a must have when it comes to relationships and child rearing.

☞ Being capable
This is a broad term and can apply to many different things, but in relationships this applies to life skills. If your partner is doing well on their own, they can hold a good job, look after themselves and other people and can keep up with their set schedule, it's a great sign. You need someone who knows how to make their way in life, not someone that you'll need to parent. You're looking for an equal. This may sound as though you are seeking an employee and not a partner, but we also need to think practically. Your future partner shouldn't set you back with their lack of life capabilities. Especially if you know you want to have kids in the future. Having a family demands a lot of capability from both parents.

☞ The relationship is moving at a comfortable pace.
It also means that your date respects your boundaries and is not pushing you into anything that feels uncomfortable. It's not the best sign if your date wants to quickly jump into a relationship, especially when you have yet to connect to them properly. If your date doesn't want a commitment and they want to hang around in the limbo phase of a casual relationship and you want to move a step further, it's also a bad sign.

Some people think they can just wait it out and love will make the other person take that next step. You are living in a fairy tale again! The truth is that some people are very comfortable in the limbo phase and by being nice, loving and understanding you're making them feel even more comfortable. Your date might be already getting all the benefits of a long-term relationship without having to commit to anything. If that's the case, it's about time you requested a change. If it doesn't work, all you can do is leave the situation, dust yourself off and go back to the fish tank! You need honest communication about your levels of commitment and the speed that you're comfortable with. Make sure your date is willing to talk and negotiate the terms of your relationship. You're on this journey together.

☞ Willing to work with you.
Please remember that perfection doesn't exist. Stop looking for a partner that will fit you in every way. Every relationship has problems. As long as your values align and you have a life path that you can take together, you only need someone who will be willing to work on it with you; someone who will accommodate your needs and will work on compromises, deals and agreements throughout life. It's a must-have green flag.

☞ Being supportive.
A good partner will have the capacity to support us, especially during hardship. It's easy to be kind and helpful when it suits us. The real test comes when life gets tough, and you are leaving the "honeymoon phase" of the relationship. So, keep this flag in mind throughout the duration of your relationship. An amazing life partner will create a space for you to be messy, sad, angry and in despair. And will be rebuilding the connection with you when the storm has passed.

* * *

I'm sure there are plenty more behaviors and qualities that could be added to the list, but I believe these are the main ones that you should be looking for. The best screening tool for red and green flags are deep and meaningful conversations. The problem with society today is that we're afraid to have them because we're terrified of getting vulnerable. If you don't get into the nitty-gritty and expect only to stay on the comfortable shallow end, you'll miss the red flags and won't appreciate the green ones either. Work on yourself, on your own depth of thought and broaden your comfort zone. If you do that and become a great thinker, you can become a great conversationalist. When you know how to infiltrate your own mind, you'll be able to infiltrate the minds of others, and this will give you a massive advantage in the dating world.

So be brave enough to get vulnerable, to get rejected and even ignored. If you can withstand this and come back like the phoenix to the dating scene just to go through everything all over again and put your heart on the line, you will truly become a great dater, partner, and a lover. It's not about a naïve belief that people will be gentle with you, so you choose to believe the goodness. No, you know already that the dating world is not easy and sometimes cruel. And despite that knowledge you choose to put yourself out there again with courage. Informed courage will keep you protected but able to find love and connection. It will allow you to ask difficult questions and not stop at simple answers.

Curiosity can be difficult for people because we might not always want to hear the answers to some deep questions that need to be asked in every relationship. The world seems to be calling for accepting differences in people, but not for differences in opinions. If you remove your expectations, simply listen, and accept that others might be very different from you, you'll find out much more about them. If you truly choose to be curious, you could learn much more about yourself and the world rather than if you listen through the filter of bias, expectations, or stubbornness.

So, stop imagining the answers and truly ask your date about it! Everything can be timed and worded in a way that isn't cruel or inappropriate, however, it can still be hurtful, but we can minimize it. Apart from having the best communication possible we're not responsible for what people feel. We of course need to be tactful, considerate and kind, but our words can still be taken out of the context and hurt others deeply. It doesn't mean that we shouldn't speak up. Those important conversations about your values, convictions and attitudes towards the world are the most important information that you should be taking away from your dates. Ultimately this is what you'll need to align with your partner if you choose to take things further.

Start getting comfortable with depth and hearing different opinions. When you do that and stop daydreaming during your dates, you'll be able to see all the red and the green flags. When you have that skill, you can navigate dating waters much safer.

Before you allow someone to become your partner, you need to gather enough information about red and green flags and perhaps yellow ones too. We went through each red flag already and there I've mentioned remedies for curing a red flag, if a red flag responds to treatment, it means it changes the color to yellow and it could potentially disappear. You need to be the judge of the color-coding here. If you state your boundaries and needs and they're fulfilled in some way, you can safely say that your date is taking to heart what you said, and they're willing to make a change for you as their partner or potential partner.

* * *

EXERCISE: Flags and Dealbreakers Accounting

If you struggle to recognize the "colors" of flags, this is an exercise for you. But let's start with general dealbreakers. From the previous chapter you should have your dealbreaker list ready. If you can see that there is no way your prospective partner is able to change them or negotiate around them, there is no point in investigating their flags. You are simply not suited for each other. Perhaps they will change their mind and values after a couple of years of a relationship or maybe they won't. If they won't change them, you will be going through a long and painful break up and will need to start looking for a new relationship all over again. Or you will need to be the one adjusting to them. It's a gamble that you will need to decide whether or not to take.

If, however, you don't see any dealbreakers, you are safe to explore the flags. In your diary create three columns or devote one to each color. Start with green flags and write down all the behaviors that your date performed such as making comments, stating opinions, gestures, making propositions and their general interaction with you. Describe what they did and what types of positive traits were displayed because of their behavior.

Next focus on red flags and do the same thing but try to analyze what negative traits were presented. Your last page or a column will be devoted to potential for yellow flags. Are any of the red flags situational? If you see that there's a bigger pattern of behavior that means, it's a strong red flag. If, however, the behavior happened once and/or there were some circumstances in which the behavior is understandable, you might consider some ways to check if a red flag could change color to yellow.

This is all very subjective so you can also ask your friends and family for an opinion. If you choose to explore the "change of color", you should use your boundaries and good communication to flesh out the meaning and gravity of a certain red flag. It's a time when you'll need to negotiate a change in your date's behavior or ask them what's wrong and how you can help them change their behavior. You can also be more direct and focus on yourself and create an external boundary or present them with future consequences of their behaviors. We can all request from others to behave around us in a certain way, within reason of course. If they deny the request or ignore you, that's the cue that there's no bleach available in this case.

If you're left with even one unchangeable red flag, it might mean that you are beginning a relationship that will suffer from issues later on, especially if you're facing narcissistic red flags.

* * *

SUMMARY

In this chapter we looked at the most common green flags. I've outlined the behaviors of the very best partners. Use this knowledge to better yourself by performing those behaviors. When you have those habits in place, it will be easier for you to acknowledge other people's good behaviors. It will also make you realize that you're not asking for too much, because you're an amazing partner with great qualities, so you deserve the same. Lastly, I've included an exercise that brings together red, yellow, and green flags so that you can analyze all those signs and behaviors. Such close analysis will help you make your final decision on whether to continue dating this particular person.

Chapter 20:
What if We Could be More than Dating?

In this chapter we discuss elements that will tell you if your prospective relationship with your date has a future. We will talk about sexual chemistry and compatibility. Next, we move on to general compatibility and finding common ground with shared values and future plans. After that, we delve into the importance of challenging one another and keeping things interesting. I will also explain what true commitment is in comparison to attachment and how we need both to sustain a relationship. Lastly, I'll explain how crucial personal growth is and choosing a partner who values it as much as you do.

This chapter is devoted to the "in between" period of time when you're both figuring out if you want to make it official or not. Going into a relationship changes the dating game. Committing to each other and promising loyalty and support is a big deal. When you're in a couple your needs can be met by your partner like by no other person, but sometimes your needs will have to wait their turn. Things become more complicated and require effort, but it can also be more rewarding. It's a constant negotiation and emotional effort, mixed with support and affection. It's not to be taken lightly. Your partner will be like a mirror for you. All of your best and worst traits and behaviors will be very visible because your other half will reflect them back at you. That's because this is the most intimate type of relation there is. Breakups happen very often, not many couples will be strong and committed enough to remain together for a long time. Divorces are very common and most of us go through at least one break up in our life. Remember that I'm talking about Western culture.

Everyone has some traits, characteristics or viewpoints that can be problematic for another person. We need to be aware that perfection doesn't exist, and we need to be looking for willing partners who will commit, fulfill your needs, or at least negotiate. Commitment to do things for one another and trust that the other person is also committed is what makes the best unions possible. You need to discuss your future as a couple. Obviously, this will evolve during the span of the relationship, but you need some assurances that your date could be a good partner for you. Remember to assess these few things outlined below before saying "let's make it official."

* * *

1. Sexual and Romantic Connection

It's important to make sure that your libidos roughly match and that you're attracted to your date. This can obviously change but it's good to have a rough idea about how important sex is to your date. For the relationship to work out, you also need mutual attraction and sexual pull. I see so many lovely couples who match at all other levels but not sexually. You can make it work with minimal sexual contact if both of you are happy with that. But if one of you craves sex more, both of you might get very depleted at some point. I meet more couples in which the woman has less craving, and the main reasons usually are lack of connection with the partner or lack of support from the partner. If your libido is decreasing, it might also be due to poor mental or physical health, stress or feeling pressure to have sex. Or perhaps you don't feel as attracted to your partner. A good sexual connection can be worked on with the help of honest conversations and creating a safe environment to share and express your sexual and emotional needs. Both partners need to be committed to making a change if you want to transform your sexual connection. Libido thrives in non-pressure, fun environment and through increasing physical intimacy in safe settings. Regular initiation without expectations for sex can also help.

2. General compatibility
You want someone who is similar enough in crucial areas and with whom there is a potential path that you can take together. To discover if you're compatible, you need to think about what you value in life. It's not about liking the same things. Partners can be very different from one another when it comes to hobbies and temperaments, but what they should have in common are values. For instance, if your partner is immersed in their work, chases money and wants professional growth and you value relationships and personal growth, you might not be compatible with one another. Values often change depending on your situation and age, so perhaps you could be compatible in the future but not right now. You need to see a path that you can take together. If you currently or in general value different things eventually those values will take precedence over your relationship. This also includes future family plans. If you want to have kids and your partner doesn't, eventually one of you will need to make a decision whether to stay and change your values or leave and preserve them.

3. Excitement
Make sure that you're different enough to keep things interesting and fresh. Someone who is similar and has nothing to bring into a relationship won't be a good fit. Great partners challenge one another in some ways. For example, you might have different knowledge, skills, or mindsets. You can discuss those and share with one another. You don't want to date a replica of yourself because you won't discover anything new which becomes boring very quickly. Make sure that you can keep the spark going in that way. Or if you're very similar, make sure that you have your individual friend groups, activities, and careers. Of course, some of those things can be joint, but if you do absolutely everything together, you can become too familiar with each other and that doesn't spark sexual tension and excitement (Perel, 2012).

4. Willingness and Commitment

Make sure that your date is willing to work with you to improve. When you enter a relationship, the arrangement between you changes, or it should if you know how to be in a healthy relationship. When you date you have a loose friendship that has romantic elements. When you decide to become a couple, the deal is that you need to support one another. That includes emotional support and practical help. You also promise to be loyal (however you define loyalty) and to acknowledge your partner while making your future plans. Often people will show commitment at the beginning and when things are going well, but the true test comes when there are issues on the horizon. There's an old Polish saying, "You will find out who your friends are when you are poor and in need." You can be a lovely couple but eventually everyone goes through some sort of hardship and needs support. A truly committed and valuable partner will stand by you and will find a way back to you after arguments and difficulties.

5. Moral compass

Do your Flags Accounting exercise and ask yourself if your date is a good person in general. Especially if you want to have a family with your partner, you need to be sure that they're a good role model for your kids or future children. If your partner displays nasty traits, mistreats others or you, they won't make a good partner for anyone. That's why I stress the importance of personal growth and morality. You cannot be in a healthy relationship or create a family if you live your life through your problematic and antisocial Parts. If you're mentally not ready to be a good person, you'll hurt your partners and children.

* * *

Spend a few minutes writing down some examples of your date's behaviors in each of these categories. It will make you realize if there's some evidence for "ticking a box" in that area. Make sure that you have attraction, connection, attachment, and commitment. Some people might be mesmerized by chemistry and strong attachment, but some relationships will simply not have enough "glue" or commitment to hold a long-term relationship or marriage. So welcome attachment, but don't mistake it for commitment, which comes later when the honeymoon period is over. That's why there are so many short-term relationships.

SUMMARY

This chapter presented you with various facets of a healthy long-term relationship. We discussed sexual and intimate compatibility and the importance of matching your sexual needs. Next, we talked about general compatibility which comes with similar life values. After we discussed what needs to be similar, I brought up the importance of bringing in different qualities into a relationship and challenging each other with your world views to keep the spark going. We also talked about the importance of a good moral compass and personal growth that both partners need to have in order to create a harmonious union and potentially a family with future kids. Lastly, I explained the difference between chemistry, attachment, and commitment. We need all of them to have a healthy and connected relationship.

CONCLUSION

Now you should have a rough idea about what to account for when deciding whether to commit to your date. The beauty and horror of love life is that we can never be sure of what will happen next. You might be thinking that this can never work at first, but then people can surprise you. Or you might be planning your future together because you're so infatuated, then the situation changes, and you break up. Don't try to control your environment, you can only control yourself to a certain degree. Explore dating life with openness but keep your wits about you and adjust accordingly to your situation, using your boundaries and following your values. Answer the questions below to establish if your date is a good and worthy partner.
1) If someone compared, you to your date would you be flattered?
2) Would you like your current, future, or imaginary child to date someone who is like your date?

3) Do you feel fulfilled with that person or just less lonely?
4) Do you feel like you can show your "true self" to this person? (This doesn't include bad communication and behavior patterns)

If the answers are "yes" and you are feeling positive about all five areas mentioned in the last chapter you found yourself a keeper!

Now you're ready for this adventure! But are you? Approach dating as a constant learning process, during which you'll find out a lot about yourself and others. Some people will come into your life for a short time and others for longer, but they'll teach you something either way. You'll exchange knowledge, views, and emotions. Some will teach you something in a positive way and some in a negative way, so try to embrace both the good and the bad. If you take on that knowledge, whatever it might be, objectively you will become richer for it.

You can use all the wisdom later in life and with new people that you meet. It's not easy to embark on the journey of self-improvement, but it will be worth it! The longer I live, the more I realize that we're not our capabilities and sets of skills, but what we believe about ourselves. Action starts with a deep belief, and we can restructure those based on the information available and our moral compass.

The moment we realize that we're all malleable, we can use that knowledge to shape ourselves into someone that we desire, like and take pride in. We can be someone who is a formidable dater and a partner. We transform very often, and it doesn't mean we are inauthentic. Authentic is also what we believe to be "us" at the core, and that can be this new transformed version that we're working on. I hope that the message that you take away from this book is:

Change your dating patterns, don't make the same mistakes, and strive for improved and healthier views, behaviors, and a better life. Take responsibility for what you do and how you date!

References

10 Commandments of Time outs in a Relationship – Terry Real homepage. (2023, March 13). https://terryreal.com/articles/10-commandments-of-time-outs/

Armitage, C. J. (2011). Evidence that self-affirmation reduces body dissatisfaction by basing self-esteem on domains other than body weight and shape. *Journal of Child Psychology and Psychiatry, 53*(1), 81–88. https://doi.org/10.1111/j.1469-7610.2011.02442.x

Banks, J., Westerman, D., & Sharabi, L. L. (2017). A mere holding effect: Haptic influences on impression formation through mobile dating apps. *Computers in Human Behavior (Print), 76*, 303–311. https://doi.org/10.1016/j.chb.2017.07.035

Barbulescu, R., & Bidwell, M. (2013). Do Women Choose Different Jobs from Men? Mechanisms of Application Segregation in the Market for Managerial Workers. *Organization Science, 24*(3), 737–756. https://doi.org/10.1287/orsc.1120.0757

Bohns, V. K., & DeVincent, L. (2018). Rejecting unwanted romantic advances is more difficult than suitors realize. *Social Psychological and Personality Science, 10*(8), 1102–1110. https://doi.org/10.1177/1948550618769880

Boser, U., Wilhelm, M., & Hanna, R. (2014). The power of the pygmalion effect: Teachers' expectations strongly predict college completion. *Center for American Progress*. http://files.eric.ed.gov/fulltext/ED564606.pdf

Bressler, E. R., & Balshine, S. (2006). The influence of humor on desirability. *Evolution and Human Behavior*, 27(1), 29–39. https://doi.org/10.1016/j.evolhumbehav.2005.06.002

Bretherton, I. (1992). The origins of attachment theory: John Bowlby and Mary Ainsworth. *Developmental Psychology*, 28(5), 759–775.

https://doi.org/10.1037/0012-1649.28.5.759

Charlson, M. E., Wells, M. T., Peterson, J. C., Boutin-Foster, C., Ogedegbe, G., Mancuso, C. A., Hollenberg, J. P., Allegrante, J. P., Jobe, J. B., & Isen, A. M. (2013). Mediators and moderators of behavior change in patients with chronic cardiopulmonary disease: the impact of positive affect and self-affirmation. *Translational Behavioral Medicine*, 4(1), 7–17. https://doi.org/10.1007/s13142-013-0241-0

Channel 4 News. (2018, January 16). *Jordan Peterson debate on the gender pay gap, campus protests and postmodernism* [Video]. YouTube. https://www.youtube.com/watch?v=aMcjxSThD54

Gottman, J. M., Coan, J. A., Carrère, S., & Swanson, C. (1998). Predicting Marital Happiness and Stability from Newlywed Interactions. *Journal of Marriage and Family*, 60(1), 5. https://doi.org/10.2307/353438
Hay, L. (2016). *Mirror work: 21 Days to Heal Your Life*. Hay House, Inc.

Jannini, E. A., & Lenzi, A. (2005). Epidemiology of premature ejaculation. *Current Opinion in Urology*, 15(6), 399–403. https://doi.org/10.1097/01.mou.0000182327.79572.fd

Judge, T. A., Livingston, B., & Hurst, C. (2012). Do nice guys—and gals—really finish last? The joint effects of sex and agreeableness on income. *Journal of Personality and Social Psychology, 102*(2), 390–407. https://doi.org/10.1037/a0026021

Kays, J. L., Hurley, R. A., & Taber, K. H. (2012). The dynamic brain: neuroplasticity and mental health. *Journal of Neuropsychiatry and Clinical Neurosciences, 24*(2), 118–124. https://doi.org/10.1176/appi.neuropsych.12050109

Kayaaltı, A., & Erbaş, O. (2021). Oxytocin, vasopressin and sexual activity. *Journal of Experimental and Basic Medical Sciences, 2*(2), 093–099. https://doi.org/10.5606/jebms.2021.75643

Kellerman, J., Lewis, X, & Laird, J. D. (1989). Looking and loving: The effect of mutual gaze on feelings of romantic love. *Journal of Research in Personality*, 23, 145–161.

Kim, S., & Labroo, A. A. (2011). From Inherent Value to incentive Value: When and why pointless effort enhances consumer preference. *Journal of Consumer Research, 38*(4), 712–742. https://doi.org/10.1086/660806

Maxwell, J. C. (2009). *How successful people think: Change your thinking, change your life*. http://ci.nii.ac.jp/ncid/BB11359429

Mayshak, R., King, R., Chandler, B., & Hannah, M. (2020). To swipe or not to swipe: The Dark Tetrad and risks associated with mobile dating app use. *Personality and Individual Differences, 163*, 110099. https://doi.org/10.1016/j.paid.2020.110099

Mellody, P., Miller, A. W., & Miller, K. (1989). *Facing Codependence: What It Is, Where It Comes from, How It Sabotages Our Lives*. http://ci.nii.ac.jp/ncid/BA36863024

Mellody, P., Miller, A. W., & Miller, J. K. (1992). *Facing Love Addiction - reissue: Giving Yourself the Power to Change the Way You Love*. Harper Collins.

Lannin, D. G., Vogel, D. L., & Heath, P. J. (2021). Reducing Help-Seeking Stigma through Self-Affirmation. In *Routledge eBooks* (pp. 56–66). https://doi.org/10.4324/9781003042464-3

Levine, A., & Heller, R. (2012). *Attached: The New Science of Adult Attachment and How It Can Help You Find--and Keep--Love*. Penguin.

Lisitsa, E. (2024, March 5). *The Four Horsemen: Contempt*. The Gottman Institute. https://www.gottman.com/blog/the-four-horsemen-contempt/

Lusignan, K. (2024). *John Gottman and Brené Brown on Running headlong into Heartbreak*. The Gottman Institute. https://www.gottman.com/blog/john-gottman-and-brene-brown-on-running-headlong-into-heartbreak/

Perel, E. (2012). *Mating in captivity: How to keep desire and passion alive in long-term relationships*. Hachette UK.

Pronk, T., & Denissen, J. J. A. (2019). A rejection Mind-Set: Choice overload in online dating. *Social Psychological and Personality Science*, *11*(3), 388–396. https://doi.org/10.1177/1948550619866189

Real, T. (2018). *Fierce Intimacy: Standing Up to One Another with Love*. Unabridged. Audio CD.

Real, T. (2022). *US: Getting Past You and Me to Build a More Loving Relationship*. National Geographic Books.

Ramaker, A. A. (2020). *The impact of the halo effect in online dating.* https://minds.wisconsin.edu/handle/1793/81376

Roland, P. (2005). *How to Meditate: Combat stress and harness the power of positive thought.* Octopus Publishing Group.

Rose, H. (2022, March 7). *The Pink Elephant Paradox: how intrusive thoughts impact our emotions and decisions.* Ness Labs. https://nesslabs.com/pink-elephant-paradox

Rosenberg, K. P. (2018). *Infidelity: Why men and women cheat.* https://openlibrary.org/books/OL26975972M/Infidelity

Scheibehenne, B., Greifeneder, R., & Todd, P. M. (2010). Can there ever be too many options? A Meta-Analytic Review of choice Overload. *Journal of Consumer Research*, *37*(3), 409–425. https://doi.org/10.1086/651235

Schwartz, R. C., & Sweezy, M. (2019). *Internal Family Systems Therapy, Second edition.* Guilford Publications.

Smith, A., & Duggan, M. (2014). On-line Dating & Relationships. *Pew Research Centre.* http://dsodown.mywebtext.org/pdf/s03-Online_Dating.pdf

STOPP Technique — ANJ Counselling & Psychotherapy. (n.d.). ANJ Counselling & Psychotherapy. https://www.anjclearview.co.uk/stopp

Tayyeb, M., & Gupta, V. (2023, June 5). *Dyspareunia.* StatPearls - NCBI Bookshelf. https://www.ncbi.nlm.nih.gov/books/NBK562159/

Timmermans, E., Hermans, A., & Opree, S. J. (2020). Gone with the wind: Exploring mobile daters' ghosting experiences. *Journal of Social and Personal Relationships*, *38*(2), 783–801. https://doi.org/10.1177/0265407520970287

Viveiros, M. (2020). Proposing the mindful check-in: a brief mindfulness exercise. *EWU Digital Commons*. https://dc.ewu.edu/cgi/viewcontent.cgi?article=1633&context=theses

Waldinger, R., & Schulz, M. (2023). *The good life: Lessons from the World's Longest Scientific Study of Happiness*. Simon and Schuster.

Wegner, D. M. (1994). Ironic processes of mental control. *Psychological Review*, *101*(1), 34–52. https://doi.org/10.1037/0033-295x.101.1.34

Wilson, G. (2014). *Your Brain on Porn*. https://openlibrary.org/books/OL27207985M/Your_brain_on_porn

Yetman, D. (2020, March 5). *Is erectile dysfunction common? Stats, causes, and treatment*. Healthline. https://www.healthline.com/health/how-common-is-ed

www.ingramcontent.com/pod-product-compliance
Lightning Source LLC
Chambersburg PA
CBHW061206070526
44583CB00025B/3134